Sugar Hill Inn

THE ART OF INNKEEPING

Thank you for staying with us.

Steven Allen

STEVEN ALLEN

Copyright © 2018 Steven Allen
All rights reserved
First Edition

PAGE PUBLISHING, INC.
New York, NY

First originally published by Page Publishing, Inc. 2018

Photography by Jumping Rocks

ISBN 978-1-64082-790-5 (Paperback)
ISBN 978-1-64082-791-2 (Digital)

Printed in the United States of America

CONTENTS

Section One—Becoming an Innkeeper
Chapter 1: What Family and Friends Say................................7
Chapter 2: The Search for the Perfect Inn............................11
Chapter 3: The Sugar Hill Inn 19

Section Two—Design
Chapter 4: Design 101..25
Chapter 5: The Money Pit..29
Chapter 6: Checking into the Dream....................................35
Chapter 7: Moving Forward..39
Chapter 8: Race to the Finish Line..45

Section Three—The Restaurant
Chapter 9: Becoming a Restaurateur....................................51
Chapter 10: Restaurant Startup—May 2006..........................57
Chapter 11: Executive Chef Val Fortin..................................65
Chapter 12: The Dining Room..71
Chapter 13: Breakfast 77

Section Four—The Good Life
Chapter 14: The Ten Reasons I Love What I Do 85
Chapter 15: Karen's Story 89
Chapter 16: Original Art 95
Chapter 17: Bartending 103
Chapter 18: Wine Adventures..109
Chapter 19: Going Local 119

Section Five—Business
Chapter 20: Core Values 129
Chapter 21: Business and the Community..........................135
Chapter 22: Being the Best in the World............................141
Chapter 23: Being Famous—Living in a Fishbowl..............147
Chapter 24: Maintenance, the Refrigeration Emergency......153
Chapter 25: Four Diamonds..159
Chapter 26: Is Airbnb a Threat to Traditional Hospitality?........167
Chapter 27: Lessons Learned 173

SECTION ONE

Becoming an Innkeeper

Chapter 1

What Family and Friends Say

The very idea of leaving New Jersey, my home of the past two decades, was unthinkable to most of the people I knew. My late wife's parents, Sara's grandparents, were particularly concerned. We had remained close in the decade since I'd been widowed. They liked having both Sara and me nearby. But amazing as it seemed to us that she could be so grown up, Sara was heading off to college out of state. And I had a grand plan of my own. My announcement appeared to be a rash, completely out-of-the-blue decision. In truth, I was acting on a long-held desire. It had been deeply buried for years, as I ran a small business close to home and raised Sara in our split-level home in a lovely New Jersey town. As she made plans to depart for art school in Savannah, I had no desire to live alone in a big house in this family-friendly suburban area.

I have always been a big believer in second acts. At the age of fifty, I had two big life goals I still wanted to achieve. This was my chance, and I meant to make the most of it. One, become proficient and knowledgeable about fine food and wine. I sold my business and enrolled in New York's famed French Culinary Institute. This was a full-immersion, life-enriching experience that was as enjoyable as it was difficult. My graduation was an achievement I will always proudly remember. The French Culinary education was an amazing ride but only step one. Set firmly on the hospitality path, I was now on to the next goal. I was going to buy an inn.

I am an unlikely innkeeper. I am an introvert, an avid traveler, and an inveterate daydreamer. None of these traits lend themselves to the realities of the hospitality business and day-to-day running of a country inn. Like many introverts, I am sensitive to my surroundings—strongly affected by view, temperature, aroma, and noise levels. Over the years, certain moments struck me powerfully, lingering in my memory bank as I went about my regular daily life as husband, father, and businessman.

The first seed may have been planted on a trip to Antigua shortly after I married. My wife and I left our resort and headed for a restaurant high up on a hill. The place was very simple. The floor was crusted stones, and the menu was basic—calling it Italian would be an overstatement. The food wasn't particularly memorable, but the views were spectacular and the ambiance warm and peaceful. The young American owner visited our table after dessert. He told us about how he gave up a successful investment-banking career in Chicago to run this spaghetti joint after falling in love with the island. I thought what he was doing was so cool. How great would it be to live in a place where most people, at best, can only vacation a week or so every year? To actually live in your own version of paradise and share your dream with others? (I also learned that his "simple" restaurant had no telephone when I asked him if he could call a taxi to take us back down the steep hillside in the dark, but that's another story.)

Every traveler lives for those perfect moments, and I enjoyed many over the years. I lingered over a perfect espresso in Rome. It was served in a perfect china cup with matching saucer and silver spoon, by a waiter in impeccable white jacket, on a sunlit patio on a terrazzo surrounded by some of the most beautiful buildings on earth. I disembarked a train in Monterossa al Mare, where a beachside café with bright-yellow umbrellas against the blue sea beckoned. The mostly Italian patrons were beautiful and happy, the beach gorgeous, the mood festive. It seemed, as I sat there, that I was in the happiest place on earth. I once bought the most delicious apple tart ever from a small patisserie in Paris that I happened to duck into. Try as I might, I could never find that place, or a tart that delicious, again. For years, I searched fruitlessly for that perfect tart—only to rediscover it in chef school in New York. But I'm getting ahead of myself.

Looking all the way back, perhaps becoming an innkeeper wasn't such a stretch. As a child I was fascinated by hotels; I remember reading biographies of hotel magnate Conrad Hilton while my friends were reading comic books and trading baseball cards. In high school, I briefly considered applying to Cornell University's famous School of Hotel Administration. I was also interested in design and considered studying architecture. These were both ideas my father quickly shot down. "With a good liberal arts degree followed by an MBA, you can do anything," he advised.

I took his advice and earned my MBA at the College of William and Mary, then entered the work world as a business analyst for a chemical manufacturer in New York. Soon enough I married, Sara was born, and our little family settled in the suburbs. When Sara's mother became gravely ill, I started my own small mail-and-parcel business just a couple of miles from home so I could always be nearby. After she passed away, raising our daughter and staying close to home were my priorities. But the past ten years had flown by, and now it was time for a very different challenge.

Chapter 2

The Search for the Perfect Inn

I remembered the many wonderful moments I'd enjoyed at various places all over the world. It was time to let my creative side out. I wanted to create my own vision of the perfect guest experience. I also wanted to buy into a lifestyle. I had visions of moving to the country, living in the beautiful mountains, enjoying my coffee on the front porch, reading by the fireplace on snowy nights, taking life a bit more slowly. This would be, I figured, almost a retirement sort of job. I thought I wanted to get away from New Jersey and slow down. I got away from New Jersey. I did not slow down.

As a man in my early fifties at the French Culinary Institute, I was definitely one of the older students. Most of my classmates were young, just beginning what they hoped would be a lifelong career as a chef. New diplomas in hand, they would be entering the kitchens of New York's finest and most innovative restaurants—as galley slaves, pretty much. They had plenty of time and energy to keep learning on the job and work their way up the ladder. I had a different dream. I had recently joined the Professional Association of Innkeepers International, known as PAII in the business, as an associate member. They offer trade shows and educational programs for both owners and those considering a career as an innkeeper. PAII also hosts an active online forum where people correspond and ask questions. A woman named Theresa posed the question one day, "Is innkeeping a suitable profession for a single person?" I wrote back and told her that while I had no actual experience, I was a single man looking to do just that. We stayed in touch through the board while I took the first real steps toward my dream. I discussed my plan with the placement director at the Culinary Institute at our required pre-graduation meeting to discuss career options. He referred me to an excellent broker in Vermont named Dick Palmer, and the two of us began our search. In my mind's eye, I pictured a gorgeous property on the edge of a cliff with waves crashing into the shoreline below, on Cape Cod, for instance. I quickly learned that oceanfront property was way out of my budget. We began a tour of realistic "possibilities."

I met Dick at the Purple Panther Inn in Manchester, Vermont. As I drove through town, I stopped to admire the stately Equinox Resort sitting proudly in the center of Manchester Village. The surrounding village with its green lawns, white picket fences, and tidy homes perfectly captured the essence of small-town New England. Among the harmonious homes and businesses, all painted New England white, one place stood out. That was where I was staying. Yes, the Purple Panther Inn really was painted a bold shade of purple. The Purple Panther didn't have a typical front desk. Instead, guests were invited to sit down in a cozy parlor room in front of the owner's desk while he handled the usual check-in details. I was shown to a small but well-appointed room with rich colors and fabrics and a gas fireplace. It was obvious that this room had been professionally decorated. Its formality and the excessive use of draped fabrics weren't quite the look I was after for my future inn, but the guestroom was certainly a pleasant place to spend a night.

The first inn Dick wanted to show me was not currently operating, which was why we were staying at the Purple Panther. In fact, Dick had recently sold the Panther to its current owner. Dick and his wife invited the new owner and myself out to dinner. I didn't talk much; I stayed very much in listening mode as I absorbed all the shoptalk about the many details of innkeeping. The next morning, after a bland breakfast, Dick and I set off for a pristine spot in the middle of nowhere. To say this inn was not currently in operations was an understatement. *Abandoned* was the word that came to mind.

It was terribly run-down, although nothing that a million or so dollars and a full year of painstaking restoration from the ground up couldn't fix. The challenge was tempting, but the reality was way beyond my means or abilities. At this early point, Dick wasn't actively trying to sell me anything. He was trying to gauge exactly what kind of properties in what condition most interested me. As we headed out of Manchester, I saw the other part of town. Just down the road a mile or two were several strip malls full of outlet stores. This was not the bucolic Vermont I was in search of; it reminded me of Fort Lauderdale, Florida, only cold. Time to move on.

The best way for a prospective buyer to see an inn is to stay the night and experience it from a guest's point of view. Because it is usually confidential that an inn is for sale, as a potential buyer, it is important to act normal. It is also customary to book and pay for your own room as any real guest would. Dick and I were off to visit another property he had recently sold so that I could meet the owners and have a tour. Our next stop, Craftsbury, was far away in the isolated Northeast Kingdom of Vermont. This inn made a great first impression. Two classic white New England homes surrounded by white picket fences were situated across a narrow lane from each other. Now this was what a New England Inn was supposed to look like. I was given a tour of all the available rooms and spent a good portion of the afternoon in the kitchen talking with Jim, the owner. Before dinner, I took a walk up the road. It was so quiet all I could hear were the sounds of nature. The remote countryside was so peaceful. I loved it. Dick and I enjoyed a pleasant, quiet dinner at the inn. Afterward, I relaxed in my room with a good book since there was no TV or Internet. The next morning I had a basic breakfast. The food was decent, but nothing that really stood out, just like breakfast at the Purple Panther. After seeing just two inns, I was thinking that I could certainly do better, at least in the breakfast department. I headed home with a much better idea of the realities of innkeeping and plenty to think about.

There were some valuation issues resulting from the sale of some property that the owners in Northeast Vermont had recently made, so I did not seriously pursue the second opportunity. The inn was never sold and eventually closed in bankruptcy. A shame. With the right owner, that property could have been a fantastic inn. Just a week after our road trip, I heard the shocking news that the Purple Panther had burned down to the ground. Nothing left but ashes. The fire was caused by excess lint buildup in the industrial dryer. A very important lesson on the road to innkeeping: attention to detail and proper insurance are critical.

Over the next few months, I took several trips north to check out inns and B&Bs and met with many different business brokers. My next trip up to Vermont was to meet a broker named Wendy Beach. Wendy was young, blond, and attractive. Unfortunately, she was also married. The first inn she showed me was down the street from Ben and Jerry's Ice Cream factory; that was very cool. It was also across the street from a shopping center, and that was not very cool. I was not moving to Vermont to buy an inn across the street from a shopping center. I wanted views, land, and nature—a property that captured the essence of rural New England.

Next, we drove all the way across the state and into Lyme, New Hampshire. Lyme could have been a movie set. There was the beautiful green commons lined with quaint New England buildings and homes with picket fences, all painted regulation New Hampshire white. At the far end of the square stood the three-story, imposing, and slightly haunted-looking Alden Inn. This property had the potential to be a fantastic boutique hotel. Currently, it was mainly a restaurant. I quickly understood why: the rooms on the upper floors of the Alden Inn were quite outdated and ordinary. Every spring, the owner literally carried window air conditioners up two steep flights of stairs to place them in the inn's windows. The location and historic building intrigued me. I was drawn to this property but knew in my heart this was a much bigger undertaking than I could handle. (My intuition was right. One day years later, I was driving to the Dartmouth bookstore in Hanover via back roads when I rediscovered the Arden Inn. A sign on the front door just said CLOSED. I wasn't surprised but felt a pang of sadness. It was closed for a few years before undergoing major renovations. It is open again, but much of its original charm has been lost.)

I was also charmed by the Highland Inn in the Lakes District of New Hampshire. The property was located on a beautiful county road with a view onto a peaceful small lake. The innkeeper was a recently divorced man. His wife left, and it had never been in his plans to run an inn by himself. He planned to return to the "real world" and resume his prior career as an engineer. Their innkeeping experiment had been heartbreaking in more than one sense. I loved the way the house sat on the land, the idyllic pond, the rustic old barn out back. Regrettably, most of the home's old architectural details were missing. The Home Depot doors with the fake wood grain and factory-applied white finish rubbed me the wrong way. Too much of the house's soul had been destroyed in a remodel.

As a young adult, I had stayed at the Golden Stage in Proctorville, Vermont, while doing a Bike Vermont Tour. I had many fond memories of that trip. When I heard that the Golden Stage was for sale, my imagination went wild, and I immediately arranged a visit. As anyone who has ever attended a class reunion can tell you, a lot can change in twenty years. A junkyard had opened across the street, and the inn was not nearly as nice as it had seemed when I was young.

Ludlow is a Vermont town where you can refuel and stock up on Dunkin' Donuts then keep right on moving. On a busy nondescript street in Ludlow, Dick and I stopped to see our next inn. My mind was already saying "No way" as we prepared to enter. I could see the owners' home—a boring 1970s-style home built in the backyard of this boring inn. I was stunned by the inside; the interiors of this inn were absolutely beautiful. The original hand-carved woodwork was exquisite. If only this place was in Woodstock, it would be worth a fortune. The next two inns I visited were both located just outside Woodstock, Vermont. The first was a small B&B with only six rooms, owned by two guys. I had learned at B&B school that for a viable business, you need at least eight rooms, and planned to stick to that advice.

Just up the road was the Jackson House, a beautiful property in every way. I stayed the night and, as usual, had dinner in their dining room with Dick and the owners. From the outside, the inn was impressive. The inside more than lived up to the outside. Each guest room was decorated with luxurious fabric and bold wall coverings. The owner's wife was an interior decorator. Although the decor was a bit overdone for my taste, it was lovely and professional. The inn also had stunning original works of art everywhere. Just over the course of our dinner, I could tell by their manner and easy conversation the innkeepers were experienced and the inn was a well-run business. Ultimately, at over $2MM, I felt that buying Jackson House was just too big an undertaking for me. I wasn't experienced enough to move right in and start running this inn, even though it was a completely turnkey operation. Everything was impeccable and running smoothly. An important element was missing: there was very little room for me to place my personal stamp on the inn. Potential owners would pay top dollar for an inn at the very peak of its glory. Though tempting, I let this opportunity go.

I took a look at the Red Shutter Inn at Mt. Snow. It was an okay property and probably could have been run as a successful business but lacked the potential to ever be anything more than just another average ski town inn. I considered placing an offer on the Westerly B&B near Sugarbush, which came very close to being all I wanted. On a beautiful piece of land, quiet and tranquil, with everything right down to their own chickens for eggs. Another buyer moved faster and made an offer first. It is now a member of Select Registry and has a very good reputation.

I had now inspected over ten inns/B&Bs that were for sale in Vermont and Southern New Hampshire. While that might not seem like many, looking for an inn is quite a different proposition than buying a house. Within any region of the country, there are only a handful of interesting properties available at any one time. The good news was that by now, I had a firm idea of exactly what I was looking for.

- A beautiful rural location and lots of land and great views
- A full-service inn where the inn was more important than the restaurant
- A turnkey investment but with ample room for growth
- A property suitable for a man, not too frilly
- A historic building

I was also seeing firsthand just how unusual it was for a straight, single man to want to become an innkeeper. They are quite an anomaly in this line of work. Running an inn or B&B attracts many single women; gay male couples owning an inn together is also commonplace, like the guys I met in Woodstock. However most inns were run by husband and wife teams. I also saw inns run by professional hired managers.

The other issue that became clear to me as I visited properties was that this was a venture that clearly burned people out — fast. Many of the proprietors who were selling had only owned their inn for three years or less.

Innkeeping sounds attractive to many accomplished Martha Stewart types, the kind of person who can do over an old house and turn it into a real showplace with gorgeous furniture and flowers and entertain beautifully and live graciously. Unfortunately, that is only part of the picture.

Too many people don't put the emphasis on the fact that you are buying a business, not a fantasy life of playing hostess in the big beautiful historic home... that you happen to share with guests. In the end it's a hard cold business, and you have bills to pay. Big bills. An inn with a restaurant, for example, means a whole business within a larger business. Most people know intellectually that when starting any small business — particularly a restaurant -- the odds are overwhelmingly against them. But it's easy to forget in the excitement of buying an historic B&B. The heart overtakes the head! I kept these cautionary tales in mind as we continued the search. Just before Christmas in 2005 Wendy called to say that her partner had just listed an inn in the White Mountains of New Hampshire, and that I needed to visit... immediately.

Chapter 3

The Sugar Hill Inn

I had never visited the White Mountains before and had for some reason always thought of New Hampshire as Vermont Lite. I could not have been more wrong. The White Mountains are more dramatic than anything Vermont has to offer. Between the Kinsman and Franconia mountain ranges lies the Franconia Notch, a mountain pass of surpassing natural beauty. Peaks, valleys, waterfalls, abundant wildlife, all surrounded by several perfect small New England villages complete with general stores. The Sugar Hill Inn was located in picturesque Sugar Hill, New Hampshire (population approximately 500). I knew immediately this was a place I could happily call home. What I loved about the Sugar Hill Inn was its potential to be great again someday. The property started as a small farmhouse built by the Oakes family in 1789. The Oakes were among the first settlers in the Sugar Hill area, a classic example of the hearty, independent folks who came to the White Mountains of New Hampshire in search of a better life. Their traditional New England house utilized post-and-beam construction and relied on handsome fireplaces in the principal rooms for heat.

In the 1920s, the current owners made a large addition to the original house. The Richardson family then began operations as the Caramat Inn. Iconic movie star Bette Davis, at the peak of her Hollywood fame, was a frequent guest until she built her own home in the area. In the 1950s, three two-room cottages were built in a cluster on a knoll just west of the main building. Some of the area's most breathtaking views could be seen from these guest rooms and porches. In 1972, the inn was renamed the Sugar Hill Inn.

The property was just what I was looking for. Oh, it had its share of issues. The roof was going, the paint was peeling, and the plumbing was ancient, and the water smelled bad—just for starters. The current owners had deferred maintenance whenever possible, and many projects had not been professionally done, leading to bigger problems down the road that would be my headaches. Still, I wasn't deterred.

These issues were all fixable. The inn was currently operating, and its possibilities were endless. Another important reality I had faced while searching for my dream property was the importance of having financial reserves. I was fortunate in the year 2006 to sell my New Jersey family home at the very top of the market, probably the most optimal month ever in terms of real estate sales. (The downside to that, the economic crash, would come later.) Selling at that exact moment was just lucky, but I knew enough not to overbuy, as in the Jackson House. The couple selling Sugar Hill Inn had put every last bit of their money into buying it, and they had no cash left to fix it up. From day one, they were behind the eight-ball, playing catch-up. He was a chef, she was a massage therapist, and they had envisioned being able to do it all themselves. They quickly realized that "doing it all" included accounting as well as being a webmaster, housekeeper/laundress, PR agent, interior designer, plumber, handyman, and chef/bartender. They were burned out. They wanted out.

I wanted in! The mountain views, the peace, the bucolic town, the starry skies at night, the perfect silence—I had found my inn. We quickly came to terms, and the sale was arranged. I was the new owner of the Sugar Hill Inn.

Having owned one small business before I knew the importance of being flexible, a problem-solver, and hopefully, a jack of all trades. Certainly, I knew it would be a bit overwhelming to have to learn all the new skills that would be required of me in my new life. I knew enough to know that I wasn't good at everything, so I'd better find some people who were!

I already had two teammates at my side. Theresa, the woman I had met online at the PAII website, and I had continued our correspondence. When it was certain the inn was mine, she wrote that she was very much interested in becoming assistant innkeeper. We met halfway between our homes at the time, had a brief meeting at a bookstore, and came to an agreement. She was there on my very first official day of work. I also had my daughter, Sara, who was a tremendous help on her vacations with everything from PR to answering the phone.

Theresa turned out to be a wise hire: she was intelligent, a quick learner, and particularly good at setting up systems. She created numerous procedure manuals for every area, such as a checklist the housekeepers needed to go through daily and weekly, or a guide to maintenance. Though I had bought an existing business, it truly was like starting over from scratch, so this skill was a great help in getting us off the ground. I was thankful to her for all she did as things got moving.

And they were moving. Not in the right direction, necessarily, but even as a brand-new owner I still had existing reservations and was taking guests. During our very first week in business, Theresa and I were having a strategy meeting with Marti Mayne, the top PR person in the B&B industry.

"You have an extremely negative review on TripAdvisor, Steve," she told me. "You need to respond to it right away."

I had never even heard of this site before. At that time, they were relatively new, not the eight-hundred-pound gorilla of the travel industry they would become. My heart sank to the ground as I read a vicious review of my brand-new baby. The water smelled, the cottage was unbearably hot, their room was infested with bees—oh, and the muffins at breakfast were too small and the weather was dreadful. Certainly, some of these concerns were valid. The inn was admittedly run-down, and though we were anxious to please, we were quite inexperienced. Still, I felt it was undeservedly harsh and completely out of my control. It certainly spurred me on to start throwing money into the pit!

SECTION TWO

Design

Chapter 4

Design 101

The negative review galvanized me. I set some ambitious goals for our first year and began refashioning the inn in my vision. The cool thing about staying at a country inn is that every establishment has its own character and personality. That personality comes from its history, location, and most importantly, the owner. When I purchased the inn in 2006, many so-called improvements were not true to the inn's historic farmhouse roots.

Although so many innkeepers believe that they are wonders when it comes to decorating, I wanted professional help. Shabby chic was not going to be my style. Top hotels, restaurants, and department stores spend millions on interior design. It's done not to feed their egos but because good design is important to their success.

While guests bring their own level of happiness, joy, and expectations to the inn, it is my job as head set designer to set the stage. Some guests come for romance, others for relaxation, and for still others, we are base camp for a White Mountain adventure.

I didn't know anyone in town yet, so I asked my attorney and banker, both of whom lived in the area and I assumed were reasonably well-off, for the best interior designer around. When they both gave me the same name, Carol Hartness, I called her immediately. She ran a charming store in Littleton, overflowing with quality furniture, gifts, and fabrics. There was no doubt she had taste and talent.

Sugar Hill had such character and personality, much of it buried under ill-advised "improvements." Its vinyl floors, industrial doors, indoor/outdoor carpet, and QVC country-hour knickknacks all offended my eyes. For those nostalgic for Grandma's house, we may have had the right look, but these were not the guests I had in mind. Authentic shabby chic was never going to be my style. We needed a look that would appeal to the next generation of inn goers.

Theresa and I spent an entire day following Carol around the inn toting large trash bags. Anything too cute (straw hats, fake flowers, signs with clever sayings, etc.) was unceremoniously tossed into the bag, never to be seen again.

I was well prepared for the remodel with numerous pages torn from *Architectural Digest* and *Pottery Barn* catalogs. I also showed Carol my favorite books on farmhouses and mountain escapes. I wanted a look that would be true to the historic old farmhouse. To me, this meant the use of natural wood, stone, and fabric. I didn't want anything overly frilly. Made in New England was my preference whenever available. We had to create an environment that was warm, welcoming, and relaxing, beautiful while authentic, and romantic yet practical (New Hampshire style feng shui!). Would I be able to verbalize my unique vision well enough for Carol to translate it into reality?

With fourteen guest rooms, plus common areas and gardens, priorities needed to be set. It was decided that first impressions were very important, and therefore the main floor would be our number one priority.

Our second priority was redoing the Peckett and Richardson Suites. These were our two best rooms at the time, but they weren't selling well. It was obvious to me that top-of-the-line luxury rooms, at a romantic getaway, needed king beds. Adding the new beds led to a complete makeover. These rooms quickly became best-sellers, telling us that there was definitely demand for high-end rooms in the White Mountains and, a year later, resulted in the Dream Cottage project.

Carol's first question was about the budget. While I understand the importance of budgets, they generally result in either overspeeding if too high and underachieving if too low. I wanted to spend enough to achieve my vision and no more.

A project of this size requires a lot of organization. Carol took a full inventory of everything that we owned, room measurements, and took pictures of every room and assembled all this data in a large notebook. We spent hours discussing the rooms, picking furniture, fabrics, wallpapers, and paints. There is nothing more tiring than selecting fabrics. At times, I found myself asking, "What room are we talking about?" when asked if I preferred the stripe over the paisley.

Decorating an inn is different from doing your personal home. It was all about the guests, not me. Our average guest spends only two days with us, so it is important that they feel immediately at home. When working from room diagrams, paint samples, fabric books, and pictures, it is sometimes hard to imagine the finished look. As the one paying the bill, of course, I have the final say, but when hiring a professional, sometimes you need to take a leap of faith and trust. The hardest part of being a business owner is knowing when to follow your own instincts and when to listen to others that may know more.

For the first year, the inn was frequently torn apart on weekdays with carpenters, painters, and wallpaper hangers and then quickly cleaned up for arriving weekend guests. The first year also involved a new roof, bar, library, landscaping, swimming pool, air-conditioning, paint, wallpaper, and many plumbing and electrical repairs.

Based on feedback from guests, I think that we were very successful in setting the stage in that first year, but so much more was still needed.

Chapter 5

The Money Pit

In 2006, what I loved about the Sugar Hill Inn was its potential to be great someday. It had fifteen acres, great views, and a farmhouse dating back to 1789. However, the roof was bad, the paint was peeling, the plumbing was old, and the water smelled bad, among other things. The prior owners had deferred maintenance when possible, and many projects were not professionally done, creating bigger problems down the road. Anyone that has ever owned an older home understands that I bought a money pit.

I set out ambitious goals for the first year. In our first year, we set out to replace the roof, air-condition the inn, build a pool, improve the landscaping, and renovate the main floor of the inn. Some of these projects took longer than planned, and all of them cost more than anticipated.

The thing about living up here is that everyone knows everyone. My lawyer referred my decorator, my decorator referred my landscaper, and my landscaper referred me to two very talented carpenters. When I first met Carl and Jeremiah, it could been an episode straight from the *Bob Newhart* show. Fans of that show certainly remember Larry, Darryl, and Darryl, the three brothers that would take on any job. Jeremiah had this full bushy beard, and Carl was an older man with long gray hair tied in a ponytail. It didn't take long to realize that looks can be deceiving, and these were two very talented men.

Their first job was to fix our rotting signpost before it collapsed. The next job was even more important. The Bickford Suite had no bathroom door. Theresa and I were too embarrassed to sell the room. How could you have a room with no bathroom door? Didn't anyone notice? This was not a job for a weekend warrior since the floor sloped in one direction and the ceiling in the other. Measuring up from the floor or down from the ceiling wouldn't work here. Also, a door from Home Depot would look seriously out of place and compromise the historic integrity of the inn. Carl and Jeremiah found the perfect period door at a savage yard. It was becoming apparent that these were no ordinary handymen. It turned out that a big project that was to take them all summer had just fallen through. This was our gain.

For the next several weeks, Carl and Jeremiah were busy fixing everything. Overhearing a discussion with our decorator, they learned that we were planning to build a bar and a library. They said, "Now this is what we really enjoy doing. The other stuff just pays the bills." Carl and Jeremiah were full of ideas. They had passion for restoring older homes and using reclaimed building materials. Carol, our decorator, found us an antique foot rail that determined the arch of the bar. They recommended using wood from an old bowling alley from Massachusetts, antique mirrors found at an architectural savage yard, and beautiful Vermont soap stone. Today, this boutique bar is loved by our guests, and it is the focal point of the Tavern Room. They were also responsible for the library. Their custom-built cabinets and bookshelves blend so well with the surroundings you would never know that they weren't original to the house. Books add such positive feelings and warmth to a room. A year later, Jeremiah would be our contractor for the Dream Cottage.

"You don't need air-conditioning in the White Mountains. We have a lovely mountain breeze." That's a lie, don't believe it. The fact is that it can get hot here. We weren't going to pull that con on our guests. The former owner had a few window units that he would install if a guest complained. Most inns and White Mountain hotels solve their air-conditioning problem with window units, but they are noisy and block the view. I remember seeing an inn here in New Hampshire where the owner, every spring, carried air conditioners up three flights of stairs and, in the fall, back down. I was certainly not going to do that. In an older building like ours, running duct work is almost impossible. We decided to install a ductless system by Sanyo. They are very energy efficient and quiet, and every room has its own controls. The first estimate of $50,000 seemed crazy, but all the others were even higher. The job took all summer. Every room had its own compressor outside, and both the inside unit and outside units needed electricity, so the electricians also spent the summer with us, ringing up huge bills.

Another big project for 2006 was a pool. The state had very strict standards for commercial pools, and most pool contractors were not interested in the job. Custom Pools won by default. The contract was full of unlikely contingences that would cost extra if they occur, and of course they did. We also wanted a hot tub, but current health regulations made it too complex. Most whirlpools used in hospitality would not meet today's health regulations.

Many innkeepers think that pools are for children and therefore have no interest in them, but that was not my vision. I pictured the pool being a quiet oasis where adults could relax, enjoy quiet conversation, and take in the view of Mount. Lafayette. This pool was inspired by my father's memory. My dad worked very hard, and his idea of a vacation was a beautiful and quiet pool to sit by with a good book. I spent hours staking out the pool to get just the right views. The waterfall into the pool lends a tranquil feel to the entire backyard. The pool is loved by our guests and validates our concept.

Tom Bartlet, a friend of Jeremiah, became our roofer. Tom, a roofer in summer, spends his winter running dog sleds. Tom's sleds were built by Carl and Jeremiah. For two weeks, Tom's big crew was everywhere.

The next problem was the water. Safety was never an issue. By law, our well is tested several times a year by the state lab. We learned that our water had high magnesium content, and that gave off a sulfur smell. Here again we were puzzled that no one had addressed this issue sooner. Culligan designed a treatment system that included carbon filtration and softening. About every three years, the activated carbon needs to be replaced at the cost of $1,000. We recently had a relapse of water issues, and solving it meant becoming a water chemistry expert. Many hot water heaters have magnesium anodes that help prevent corrosion and therefore extend the life of the water heater. However, if you run softened water through such a system, the anodes add too much magnesium to the water, causing the hot water to smell. The magnesium anodes have been replaced, and the water tastes and smells great.

If our efforts were to pay off in increased occupancy, we had another problem. Much of the inn's basic infrastructure could not handle more guests. Reservations took too long to process, the kitchen had no ice machine or even a working dishwasher, and the laundry facilities were inadequate. All these problems were also fixed in the first year.

As the cool winds of November began blowing, Carl and Jeremiah were winding down their work for the season. Winter was ski season, and they would not be available again until next spring.

Chapter 6

Checking into the Dream

March 2007, my guests loved the inn as it was, and that was why they were my guests. Many had been coming here for years. They were okay with an inn that was rough around the edges in exchange for lower rates. This was not an uncommon strategy—to cut costs to the bone, defer maintenance, keep the staff small, and work like crazy—among White Mountain lodging properties. However, that business model offered no hope of ever turning a profit and had failed the previous owners.

With an embarrassingly low occupancy rate, only an optimistic dreamer would be thinking about adding new capacity. Part of the problem was that there was an oversupply of good but ordinary rooms in the White Mountains, and we had to take a risk and do something remarkable to have any impact in this marketplace. The success of the newly renovated suites led us to believe that there may be opportunities for upscale accommodations.

I wondered to myself, where did the fans of the Ritz-Carlton stay in the White Mountains? Or maybe New Hampshire was just not one of those markets that attracted the luxury traveler. As an entrepreneur, I went with my gut feeling that there was room at the top of the market for a one-of-a-kind, remarkable room. Only time would answer the age-old question, If I build it, will they come?

At that time, our cottages, in spite of being dated, were more popular than similarly priced but nicer rooms within the inn. The idea of a cottage in the White Mountains seemed to capture the yearning for a cozy escape from everyday life. I was going to venture in somewhat uncharted waters by combining cozy comfort with luxury.

The secret of a country inn, when compared to a new hotel or motel, is that every room has heart, personality, and history. There is something magical there that can't be explained in words. In the 1789 farmhouse, those warm feelings are everywhere, but extending them to new construction was going to be a challenge. In getting it right, I spent hours studying books on New England farmhouses, country cottages, bungalows, and mountain escapes. I wanted to understand the essence of each type of structure. What makes a farmhouse tick and what it is that draws people to mountain escapes. The last thing that I wanted to build was a Disney-themed room. The new structure had to be authentic and timeless in its appeal. The authenticity was to come from the use of natural material such as wood and stone and respecting the traditions of New Hampshire architecture.

The inspiration for the room came from my daydreams. I pictured french doors opening to an amazing view, a cathedral ceiling, porch swing, viewing a roaring fire from the luxury of a tub for two. With the oversize walk-in shower with body sprayers, rain head, etc., and Swedish sauna, I wanted to take the room beyond romantic and into the realm of being very sexy but tasteful.

The first decision was to hire Jeremiah. Jeremiah had built our bar and the library bookshelves. He was a craftsman, not a contractor. He was passionate about making the Dream Cottage a work of art. At every opportunity, he added extra detail beyond the scope of the project. Mikel Smith, our tile-and-stone guy, was also an artist. Watching Mikel build the chimney by selecting just the right stone and carefully putting it in place was fascinating.

To visually tie the cottage to the inn, the cottage was clad in white wood siding, just like the main inn. The use of vinyl siding was totally rejected. Wide plank pine that closely matched the original 1789 flooring on the second level of the inn was used. The stonework on the chimney, outside posts, foundation, and fireplace closely matched the inn's stone work.

The room also had to be romantic. Most hotel rooms, even expensive rooms, are more functional than romantic. We like to focus on cozy places for two, mountain views, warm fireplace, soft robes, soothing whirlpools, and relaxing saunas.

By industry standards, we spent way too much on construction and furnishing; however, hindsight told us that we were right to defy conventional wisdom. This is the hard part about being an entrepreneur. If you don't follow the crowd and succeed, you are a genius for thinking out of the box, but if you fail, you are a dope for not following tried and true. Of course, sometimes you are just lucky.

The cottage opened for business in late September 2007. The very first TripAdvisor review was so-so, and we were concerned. As it turns out, the room has been wildly successful. The cottage has become very popular for honeymoons and marriage proposals.

So, have we attracted the Ritz-Carlton traveler? Well, not really, and when they do come, they prefer the traditional luxury of the Peckett and Richardson Suites. However, the cottage is very popular with successful young professionals who value their time away together.

Aside from being our best room in terms of price and occupancy, it has benefited the inn in ways that are harder to quantify. As a result of the cottage, we have been written up in *Every Day with Rachael Ray* Magazine, became *Yankee Magazine*'s editor's choice, earned "Best of New Hampshire," and featured in *Cottages and Bungalows*. Some people might say that we have been lucky to get such great press coverage. And that might be true. However, if we had done the ordinary, we would not have had the opportunity to be lucky.

Chapter 7

Moving Forward

The first two years at the inn was a whirlwind of activity. We painted the inn, the roof was replaced, a new pool was added, the Dream Cottage was built, the Richardson and Peckett Suites were updated, and the main floor of the inn was redecorated, including the custom-built bar in the tavern and the custom bookshelves in the library. We also air-conditioned the inn. I can't believe that so many lodging properties in the North Country are still using noisy window units.

While most of the inn felt very dated, I needed to focus on toning down the ugly. There were things that offended my eyes. With the opening of the pool, the appearance of the backside of the inn was now an issue. Three huge industrial doors made the inn look like a rooming house. Just replacing these with raised panel doors with glass panes at the top softened the look of the inn and made a huge difference. The cottage rooms had these cheap motel doors from the fifties. Replacing these transformed the outward appearance of these rooms from low-income housing to cute.

The next "cheap motel" issue that needed immediate attention were the bathrooms with vinyl floors and cheap shower surrounds. This meant the Blue, Rose, and Moses rooms in the main inn and all the regular cottage rooms. Since cottage rooms were in need of a complete renovation, we started with Blue and Rose. Blue and Rose, being in the original farmhouse with their two-hundred-year-old wide plank floors, were our most traditional rooms, and for many guests, these rooms captured the essence of what a New England country inn should be. Our decorator recommended that we use the white subway tiles for the bathroom walls. These can be found in so many older homes, and yet they are still so popular in new construction. Giving rooms a timeless feel is very important to my decorating sense. For years, the traditional hotel bathrooms meant a standard tub with shower above. They were functional but offered neither a superior shower nor bath experience. The new boutique hotel chains like Aloft and very high-end hotels like the Boston Harbor have gone almost exclusively with showers. Many upscale properties offer both, like our Richardson, Nickerson, and Peckett Suites and the Dream Cottage. When Karen and I travel, these are the kinds of details that we are observing. For Blue, we did just a shower, and in Rose, stayed with the traditional setup. To add a pop of color, I found these hand-painted glazed tiles of moose and bear by a New Hampshire artist that can be seen through Blue's thick, clear shower doors. To this day, housekeeping swears at me when cleaning the Blue Room. Clear glass shower doors require perfection and are very difficult to maintain.

Hexagon floor tiles are a classic look for older homes, and I found the most beautiful marble hexagon floor tiles that we used in both Blue and Rose. Yes, standard ceramic would have been a fraction of the price, but I have a thing for beautiful tile. We would revisit these rooms again in the future to improve lighting, furniture, window treatments, and art. It was first in Blue as a romantic inn that we decided that love seats would be preferable in most of our rooms over the AAA-recommended guidelines of two chairs.

For the Moses bathroom, I selected natural stone travertine. Natural stone is a way of bringing New Hampshire's mountains inside. While the bathroom is small, it is striking in its beauty. However, we had one dilemma we had to resolve. The bathroom had this wonder antique sink that was the frequent source of complaints. It was one of those old-fashioned sinks with separate cold and hot water faucets. Fortunately, a web search found an adaptor that not only solved the hot/cold issue but also looked really cool.

At this point, we felt that we had been working so hard, but there was so much more to do. If we were a chain hotel, where every room looked alike, the renovation would have been easy but boring. We continued renovating room after room.

Our decorator was given the task to update Nickerson and Moses. Down came the old-fashioned, dated flowered wallpaper. In Nickerson, the queen bed was replaced with a king. Kings are perceived as both more romantic and luxurious. So over time, we have replaced all the queens where room size permitted. The Nickerson bathroom, although substandard, would need to wait a couple more years to be addressed. Because of the expense, the time to plan, and the need to focus on the everyday management of the inn and restaurant, progress could be made only so fast.

Karen said after seeing the bill for Moses, "You spent what? We need to be our own decorator." From that point on, Karen and I worked together on interior design issues. Karen loved fabrics, was a perfectionist when it came to painting, and understood how good lighting could make a statement. It was not uncommon for Karen and me to sit together with the newest issue of *Architectural Digest* and to discuss the projects page by page. Under my desk was always a huge pile of *Restoration Hardware*, *Pottery Barn*, and *Front Gate* catalogs for inspiration.

The Wildflower/Perennial Cottage was our next project. The cottages were originally built in the 1950s as motel units. In the 1950s, it was cool to stay at a motel. At that time, these buildings had flat roofs. When the motel novelty wore off, a pitch roof was added, turning the motel units into cottages. These rooms were terrible. The bathrooms had cheap shower surrounds, vinyl floors, and were way too small. The bedrooms had indoor-outdoor carpeting, ugly furniture, and cheap painted paneling. In spite of these problems, these rooms had potential. These rooms had beautiful views of Mt. Lafayette and were cute from the outside, and guests liked the idea of staying in a cottage. We solved the bathroom space issue by removing the closet, and we solved the lack of a closet by having a beautiful custom-made antique wardrobes built to our specification in Quebec. Beautiful hickory floors and natural stone travertine gave these rooms a timeless feel. I was thinking that if you got lost on the back roads of Provence, this was what you might discover.

Year after year, we selected the two to three rooms in the most need of renovation or where a face-lift would have the most impact. Progress was not always even and steady. A design flaw in the Dream's fireplace ruined the room's window treatments. We had to add an electric vent to the fireplace, replace all the window treatments, and had the room professionally cleaned. Some projects, like widening the driveway, just needed to be done for safety's sake.

We could see the light at the end of the tunnel, but more needed to be done. All this work was not just about selecting furniture, paint colors, and fabrics. In reality, we were defining what the Sugar Hill Inn would become. Seeing the transformation was very rewarding.

Chapter 8

Race to the Finish Line

By 2011, the inn was gaining an excellent reputation as the place to stay. We had great press and strong reviews; however, not all the rooms had been renovated. We were vulnerable to negative reviews and therefore had to work quickly to finish the remaining rooms.

At first, the newly redecorated rooms were a bonus. Based on our room rates and reputation, nobody was expecting anything fancy. However, by 2011, we had a problem. The inn was developing a fantastic reputation. *Rachael Ray* magazine wrote a story on the Dream Cottage, *New Hampshire Magazine* had featured us in two articles, we earned the *Yankee Magazine*'s Editors' Choice Award, and had excellent reviews. We were also listed in *1000 Places to See Before You Die* (USA). So what was the problem? We had a secret. Not all the rooms were great. We took the renovation of the inn seriously so that there was a huge difference between the renovated rooms and the others. We needed to act fast to correct this inconsistency. Unfortunately, we did suffer a couple of negative reviews. The very last people to stay in Nickerson before we redid the bathroom wrote a very mean review and posted photos of the bathroom. While the old bathroom was not pretty, his photography made it look ten times worse. In my response to the review, I proudly announced that the bathroom had been completely renovated since their visit. The new bathroom included a large walk-in shower, a marble-top vanity, and beautiful tile work.

In early November of 2011, after our busy season, we stayed at our favorite hotel in Quebec City, Auberge Saint-Antoine. The bathroom had the feeling of a spa. It was the combination of the layout, the spaciousness, and the shade of green. That green became the paint color for Bickford's bathroom. Bickford was Karen's project. She selected the fabrics and furniture. Karen also stripped the wallpaper, painted and sowed the window treatments and bedspread with sensational results. Accent lighting, a delightful window seat, gas stove, and a beautiful watercolor by Debbie Aldrich completed the room. In the winter, when not rented, this room is Karen's secret retreat. On that same trip to Quebec City, Karen and I purchased a new painting for Nickerson Suite and saw two others that we would keep in mind for our next project.

In late winter of 2012, we were almost at the finish. The only major project still needing serious attention was the Forest View/Garden Cottage. For inspiration, we decided to spend a couple of nights in Portland, Maine. There are so many everyday details to running an inn that taking a step away helps to see the big picture and stimulates creative thinking. Portland is a wonderful city with great restaurants, art galleries, and shops. We stayed at the Danforth B&B, in a beautiful residential neighborhood of Victorian homes a couple of blocks from the center of town. At Company C, we saw contemporary furnishing with bold, fresh colors and textures. In the port area, there was a fantastic tile store where we saw the latest trends in tile. We also visited lots of galleries, cooking stores, and had a great dinner at Five Fifty-Five.

Feeling relaxed and full of ideas, we headed back to New Hampshire. We were going to have a friendly competition. Karen would design Garden, and I would design Forest View. Karen had the insight to understand that so many of today's guests were tired of the Victorian or country look found in so many B&Bs and therefore would make Garden our most contemporary room. In many ways, Karen and I are much more influenced by what our colleagues in the boutique hotel industry are doing than our fellow innkeepers. This room with its espresso-stained built-ins, gorgeous granite counter, sleek fireplace, track lighting, and original art makes a bold statement. Karen also did the painting and made the window treatment. Don't confuse homemade with being an amateur. Karen's workmanship is totally professional in every way. If you don't have the talent, call in the pros.

People come to New Hampshire to enjoy the great outdoors. The state is famous for not only its mountains but also its lakes. I wanted Forest View to be in harmony with nature. Forest View was going to have the look and feel of a New Hampshire lake house. At Restoration Hardware, I found a large wardrobe and bathroom vanity in weathered driftwood oak. Keeping with the theme, the love seat was made from seagrass, and the rug, in an abstract way, captured the pristine blue-green colors of a mountain lake. Natural whitewashed wood floors worked perfectly with the other elements. Many people have told me that the walk-in shower reminds them of a waterfall. Tying all the elements together was a wonderful original landscape painting of a lake with mountains in the background.

Beyond the usual hotel accessories, we like to add some fun items to our rooms, such as games and interesting books. While visiting my daughter in New York City, we stopped into a great independent bookstore. I discovered this book, *Poolside with Slim Aarons*, by Slim Aarons. Slim Aarons is a very famous photographer. The book has beautiful photos of jetsetters and their glamorous swimming pools. I spent twenty minutes studying the photos page by page. And yes, there were a few topless photos from the French Riviera. It occurred to me that the book fit well with the theme of the cottage, and maybe our guests might equally enjoy a twenty-minute escape with the book.

For innkeepers, there is no clear delineation between work and play. We had several shopping trips to the lakes region and beyond in search of the perfect items for these rooms. I enjoyed our trip to the stone yard to select the granite for Garden. It is amazing how the stone is transformed from a rough slab to a beautiful countertop. As a side note, I find it puzzling that New Hampshire is the Granite State and there is no commercially available granite for sale from

New Hampshire. We had other trips to select floors, cabinets, and other items. These shopping days were usually combined with lunch. These were fun days for Karen and me.

Each of these rooms in their own way is strikingly beautiful. If you are on a weeklong trip across New England, staying in five or more places, these rooms will stand out for their uniqueness. The best part is that these rooms are priced as standard rooms. Standard does not mean average at the Sugar Hill Inn. If you are wondering who won the competition, the prize goes to Karen. Out of fourteen guest rooms, Garden is the second most-booked room, and Forest View is the fifth most booked. When I am joking around with guests at the bar and talking about the competition, I explain away my loss by saying, "Karen spent more." And while it is true that she spent more and her room is beautiful, the real difference is that she had the insight to understand what today's guests want. Marriot pays big bucks to hospitalities professions with Karen's keen intuition.

Yes, we were done with the big stuff, but keeping an inn relevant and fresh is a never-ending job. For now, we are in the refining and polishing mode. At some point, another Dream Cottage secluded deep into our fifteen acres would be the perfect addition to the Sugar Hill Inn.

# SECTION THREE

The Restaurant

Chapter 9

Becoming a Restaurateur

I don't understand it, but I am a restaurateur. I own what many think is the best restaurant in the White Mountains. Besides some momentary fantasies, I never envisioned myself owning a restaurant. Life has so many twists and turns that defy the best of plans.

The restaurant is a tale of two men, the executive chef Val Fortin and myself. In all honesty, our executive chef Val deserves most of the credit. I will go into great detail about Val in a later chapter, but for now, let's begin with my story.

My interest in food began in my childhood. Both of my grandfathers were in the food business. Food in my family was talked about more than the weather. We were experimenting with avocado, asparagus, artichokes, and heart of palm long before the food network or Julia Child made these items popular. My parents would never visit a fast-food restaurant. My mother would always grind her own hamburger meat. I was a freshman in college the first time I went to a McDonald's, and I learned that ground beef at a fast-food restaurant does not automatically cause food poisoning.

My dad was in the chemical industry with an office in New York City. Since the products were abstract and there were no tires to kick, business was frequently done at lunch. The late fifties and early sixties were the days of the three-martini lunch. Although, he was always smart enough to keep sharp while others were overdoing it. My mother would frequently join them for the important clients that were entertained at dinner. Just like Darin and Samantha on *Bewitched*. The next day, my mother would tell me all about what she ate and how it was served.

I was an early fan of the *Galloping Gourmet* and *Julia Child* and would watch them with my mother. The way Graham Kerr ran around the kitchen with a glass of white wine made cooking look fun. Doing chores around the house was part of my childhood. While my brother preferred to help Dad with the yard work, I preferred to help in the kitchen.

My parents traveled on business a lot to Europe in the late fifties and early sixties and were exposed to a food culture that had not developed yet in the States. After a trip to Switzerland, my father, who never cooked, made us a cheese fondue. He approached it with the precision of a scientist. They had also discovered white asparagus and liquors such as Grappa.

On school vacations, as a family, we would spend a day in New York City. My father would go to his office, and my brother, Jeff, Mom, and I would go sightseeing or shop and join my father for lunch at a nice restaurant. Around the corner from my dad's office was Giambelli's Restaurante located on Madison at 37th Street. Many of the dishes were prepared table side, and my eyes were glued on the show. The maître d' in those days was so well trained. Neatly filleting a whole fish table side while being watched is a long-lost skill at all but the most expensive restaurants. They would always make veal piccata with artichokes for my mother even if it was not on the menu. No way was I going to eat from a children's menu. If it wasn't good enough for my mother, I was not interested.

When I was about twelve, I discovered the recipe for veal picatta in *Gourmet Magazine*, and I cooked my first real gourmet meal. Over the years, I would make this recipe hundreds of time. This first recipe taught me that great food requires quality ingredients and careful preparation. I discovered an Italian butcher shop that would cut the veal very thin. Supermarket veal was way too tough for this dish. I studied the recipe intensely and followed the instruction precisely. I would pound the veal even thinner, add salt and pepper to flour and lightly dust it. This was long before animal rights activists had a problem with veal. I would sauté my veal a few pieces at a time until lightly golden on both sides. The smell of the butter and olive oil cooking together was heavenly. The next steps were deglazing the pan with white wine, adding fresh lemon juice and thin lemon rounds. Because the pan still had some residual flour, these ingredients formed a light sauce. The artichoke hearts and the veal would be added back until hot.

In high school, I learned of the Culinary Institute of America (CIA) in Hyde Park, New York, but I was not encouraged to attend. This was long before it was cool for a guy to go to cooking school. Instead, I followed the path of least resistance, earning a liberal arts degree followed by an MBA degree. For the next thirty years, cooking would be just a hobby and a part of everyday life.

When my daughter, Sara, was in high school, we would from time to time take classes at the Natural Gourmet Cooking School in New York City. After my wife passed away, I became a vegetarian for a while, and this school had wonderful classes. There is a lot more to vegetarian cooking than just pasta. Their curriculum also included fish and healthy meats. They also offered a six-month professional chef program, and I decided that taking the program would be a fun thing to do and most likely useful before buying an inn.

The Natural Gourmet School was taking a long time to process my application, so to play it safe, I interviewed at the French Culinary Institute.

The walls of the main hall in the French Culinary Institute show off portraits of former students. "This is Bobby Flay . . . one of our first students . . . Oh, and Jacques Pepin is on the board. He often does cooking demos," my guide pointed out casually. It was all very heady stuff. This was the Harvard of the cooking world. Who wouldn't want to go there? There was an application process and some hefty fees, of course, but the school encouraged diversity, and I was in.

I was surrounded by students of all ages, from every possible background, with varying abilities and experiences. Working next to me on my left was an eighteen-year-old girl straight out of high school and a high-powered attorney in her thirties reconsidering her original plan to become partner in a law firm on my right. The work was sink or swim. You could either do the work or you flunked out—fast. Being a fine French cooking school, the names of the dishes were naturally in French, which was a challenge for somebody who had no talent for languages and had last attempted Spanish in high school. I quickly realized that the way I pronounced words in my mind bore no resemblance to actual French pronunciation. Mastering the bare bones of French was maybe the most difficult part of the entire experience. The course itself was intense; we were on our feet all day, every day, a completely immersive experience. We would do more in six months than those junior-college programs did in two years. The goal of the program was to train chefs for five-star restaurants. These were not recipes that you would do for family. Technique was everything.

There was only one right way to do something. The answer to every question was "Yes, Chef!" If you were working on something and you were asked, "What is this?" you knew that you had screwed up, and no answer would be correct, and it was time to start again. It was important to come to school prepared. I commuted to the city from Jersey and would read my assignments and review the recipes for the day on the train. We had frequent written tests. I would remake many of the recipes at home on the weekends. You needed to be totally open to all kinds for food because we cooked everything. As all chefs do, we each owned our own set of tools. We had fantastic access to the highest quality food and ingredients, which was a real treat; we worked in the school's restaurant, one of the best French restaurants in New York City. Today the school has expanded its curriculum and is known as the International Culinary Center.

Sara came to my graduation celebration and was very proud of dear old dad. Along the way, I rediscovered that long-ago apple tart that I had been searching for and mastered its secrets.

The course was a memorable life experience, and although I loved learning about food and enjoyed the school, I did not want to spend all day in the kitchen and make a career of being a full-time chef. I would need to wear the chef's hat as part of my duties for a while, at least, among many others.

As I discussed in an earlier chapter, I took a weekend class in innkeeping. In the class, I learned that inns with restaurants generally are no more expensive than a bed-and-breakfast with an equal number of rooms. There is good reason for this. Country inn restaurants generally don't earn much and consume tons of time. Seasonality and the lack economies of scale are responsible. If you are in a community with lots of great places to eat, such as Napa Valley, California, there is no need to reinvent the wheel. Inns run restaurants because great restaurants help to sell rooms. This is especially true in rural setting. Guests can enjoy a great bottle of wine and not worry about finding their way back to the inn on dark and unfamiliar roads.

When I was looking for the perfect property to buy, I was primarily focused on the lodging side of the business. I avoided properties that were primarily restaurants and had only a handful of rooms.

At the time I purchased the inn, it was serving primarily to inn guests on the weekends. The exception was during the busy fall season when dinner was served nightly. The prior owner was a professional chef with a good reputation. Their focus was on a moderate-priced New England country food.

My offer to buy the inn was accepted in January 2006, but the closing was not until early May. This gave me four months to reenvision the Sugar Hill Inn. Although it had been an inn since 1929, the new Sugar Hill Inn would be so different it felt like a new startup instead of just a change of management. I did not want to run just an average inn and restaurant. I knew that the turnaround would not be easy and would take time. I spent a good portion of that time planning and perfecting a new menu.

Chapter 10

Restaurant Startup—May 2006

It is now a forgotten fact by everyone but me that I once was the dinner chef at the Sugar Hill Inn. As I look back, I feel good about how I met the challenge and very pleased that my leaving made way for Executive Chef Val Fortin. Everybody liked my food, but they love Val's even more.

The former owner was the chef, and he was leaving upon the closing of the contract. The restaurant served mostly to inn guests on the weekends and didn't have a strong local following. Being a small restaurant, he was the restaurant. Maybe it wasn't even really a restaurant, just a country inn dining room. There was no team of assistant chefs or cooks to stay on. The contract called for all food items to be removed and the kitchen to be thoroughly cleaned. We were starting from scratch. Originally we were going to close the contract on a Friday, but when I learned that there were guests with dinner reservations, I pushed the closing date back to Monday. I was going to need at least a few days to restock the kitchen and prepare for the first diners.

Opening a new restaurant can take months of planning and thousands of dollars. I didn't have the luxury of time on my side; I had dinner reservations on the books. Aside from the restaurant, I had an inn to run. Simultaneous to starting up the restaurant, we were doing serious renovations to the inn and replacing an antiquated reservation system.

While I didn't have answers for everything, I did have a vision for my restaurant. We would serve a leisurely dinner in a romantic setting with professional service using quality ingredients prepared fresh with proper technique. To that end, I developed a small menu that I felt confident I could execute with precision and to the highest standards. I was laying a solid foundation for future growth. As the restaurant became busier and I became more experienced, we would build a staff and could grow the menu. Even today we are sometimes criticized for not having enough selection. However, a large menu for a small restaurant is always a bad sign.

The White Mountains are not famous for nightlife. So a great meal followed by a private party back at the room is the night's entertainment for many guests. That is what fine dining is all about. You need to think about fine dining as something to experience, just like going to the theater. Imagine a musical with multiple acts building up to a conclusion and sending you home humming. Our four-course dinner guides you through a culinary experience. Add great conversation and wine with someone you love for the perfect night. We have been asked for al la carte many times, but we know that it would not deliver the same experience. The other thing that sets apart fine dining is that each dish is a totally composed creation. Broiled salmon on a plate with a choice of vegetables and starch is not fine dining. It is about a composed dish where each element contributes to the whole creation. Asking for the sauce on the side is like asking Van Gough to not use blue paint so that you could add just the right amount yourself. For maximum enjoyment, you need to trust the chef.

Having only two choices for each course has the challenge of offering food that is widely enjoyed without appealing to the lowest common denominator. I was determined that everything must be made from scratch, beautifully presented, with layers of flavor, and every course must be special and each dish executed with proper technique and precision. Although I have not been the chef in over eleven years, so much of the basic concepts and principles have endured.

Below is one of my first menus.

Four Course Prix Fixe
May 2006
Dinner Menu $45
Appetizers
Ten Spice Barbecue Shrimp Cocktail
with roasted corn—jicama salsa and crispy tortilla strips
Homemade Porcini Mushroom Agnolotti
Ravioli from the Piedmont region of Italy served with sage butter
Spring Salads
Warm Goat Cheese Salad
Basil and Arugula Salad with Melting Tomatoes
Entrées
Pan-Seared Salmon with Crispy Skin
Served on a bed of sautéed baby spinach with beurre blanc sauce
Steak Au Poivre
A filet mignon steak served with a pepper corn cognac sauce
and rosemary new potatoes
Desserts
Homemade French Apple Tart
with vanilla bean ice cream
Warm Chocolate Brownie
with cherries, vanilla bean ice cream, and brandy sauce
Coffee or Tea

Appetizers

A traditional shrimp cocktail is boring. So 1965! But adding my ten-spice mix and sautéing in the shell to impart flavor and the roasted corn and jicama salsa made it unique and complete. It was plated in a margarita glass and garnished with crispy tortilla strips for height and visual effect.

The alternative, homemade porcini mushroom agnolotti was also a big hit. The pasta was light and delicate. In a four-course dinner, it is important for the early courses to create anticipation and not overwhelm later courses.

Spring Salads

In many restaurants, the salad course is free with any entrée, and very little thought goes into it. I think that the salad course should be as special and tasty as any other course. At this point, I don't remember the exact details as to the greens, but I never forget the goat cheese. Picture a slice of the best French bread you can find with local goat cheese on top and put under the broiler until golden. The other salad was made special by the warm roasted cherry tomatoes and local basil, and the arugula was grown in Sugar Hill.

Entrées

Salmon, frequently, when served out is overcooked and boring and ordered as the healthy alternative to what you really want. My salmon had this wonderful crisp skin and was served on a bed of baby spinach with beurre blanc sauce. For perfection, make sure the raw fish is completely dry, and generously salt the flesh of the fish but never the skin. Add oil to a sauté pan and watch carefully for the first hint of the oil smoking and add the fish skin down. If the pan is not hot enough, the fish will stick, and you will have a mess. As the fish releases the fat from under the skin, lower the heat a bit. When the skin is crisp, flip the fish and place in the oven for a few minutes. The fish will emerge from the oven cooked to perfection.

To make the beurre blanc sauce, reduce one-half cup dry white wine and one-fourth cup white-wine vinegar with a tablespoon of finely minced shallots down to a couple of tablespoons. Reduce heat and slowly stir in cold butter a little bit at a time. If you do it right, you will have a wonderful white sauce. If not, it will be just a pot of melted butter.

Everyone loved the filet mignon. Just like today, we bought the whole tenderloin and hand cut and tied our steaks. Many people tell us that it is the best beef they have ever tasted. I love French cooking, and it's the sauces that make everything so delicious. The foundation of most French sauces is veal stock. While Chef Val has changed the finishing sauce over the years, the underlying veal stock is the same. Very few restaurants still make their own stocks. This is something that we have always done. The process begins by roasting veal bones. Add the roasted bones, mirepoix (onions, carrots, and celery), bouquet garni (mixture of herbs), chopped tomatoes, tomato paste, garlic, and water to a stock pot and simmer eight to twelve hours. There are a few more steps, but that is the general idea.

The potatoes and arugula were grown in Sugar Hill at Turtle Ridge Farm, and the basil was from our garden. While this was long before we were "certified local" or were a member of the Farm to Restaurant Connection, we instinctually focused on serving local when possible.

Dessert

No dinner is complete without dessert. The beauty of a prix fixe menu is that it sets a pace that allows most guests to reach the promise land of desserts. In my book, a dessert menu that features both a chocolate and apple dessert is always a winner.

Many years earlier while a student and visiting Paris, I discovered the perfect apple tart. For years I searched for an apple tart as perfect as I remembered, without success. At the French Culinary Institute, not only did I rediscover that tart, I learned how to make it. There are three simple steps that need to be executed with precision. (1) The dough is made in the traditional method of cutting ice-cold butter into flour. A food processor makes this task easy. Add a little bit of ice water with the machine running and dough will form. Wrap in plastic wrap and chill before rolling out and fitting the tart pan. It's very important to dock the shell all over with a fork. (2) An apple compote layer is added on top of the shell. It is very important that all the moisture has been cooked out of the compote. (3) Next with perfection, thinly slice the apples and artistically arrange, overlapping on top of the tart. Brush with butter and bake until golden.

The warm liquid center made the brownies very decadent. Some people call these lava cakes. A rich ice cream will add to the enjoyment. I recommend venturing beyond vanilla.

Fortunately, the dinners were well received. One guest that was hosting a graduation dinner for their daughter was concerned that the old chef was no longer at the inn. I said that I understood, and if they wished to cancel, it would be okay. They chose not to cancel and afterward told me how happy they were with everything. Another guest told me confidentially that we were not charging enough for a meal of this quality.

On days that we had guests for both breakfast and dinner, I would arrive at the inn no later than 7:00 a.m. To be ready for our 8:00 a.m., breakfast I would need to be sure that both the muffins and bacon were in the oven no later than 7:30 a.m. After breakfast, I would start making the desserts and doing the other necessary prep work. It was important to plan carefully so that everything was ready by 5:00 p.m. At that time, I would clean my station and organize everything (mise en place) I would need for the dinner service. By the time the last order went out, it was a long day. In many ways, professional cooking is like a sport. It is fast paced, requires total focus and strategy to keep everyone happy and making it to the finish line. On days I was cooking, it was up to the assistant innkeeper to run the inn. Being the dinner chef was a full-time job.

I have to say, I did enjoy being the chef, but it was not sustainable. Innkeepers in general are a talented group, and many feel that there is no job they can't do and feel the financial pressure to do everything themselves. Those are the inns that are for sale in three years. They are burned out, and they did not build the team required for long-term growth. So I decided to fire myself as chef and focus on the big picture. At about the same time, I also fired myself as the head bookkeeper. These decisions lead to building the team that would totally transform the inn.

Chapter 11

Executive Chef Val Fortin

That first year, it was a rare day that I took time off from the inn for myself. I had about four hours on a beautiful mid-August afternoon, and I decided to hike the Falling Waters Trail. The trail leads to a series of dramatic waterfalls and eventually to the top of Franconia Ridge. I explored the waterfalls but did not make it all the way to the top. The hike gave me time to think about the big picture and to analyze our progress. For most of the hike, I was pondering my role as chef. The fall was coming, and under prior management, the restaurant served seven days a week in peak season. Somewhere on the way up, I decided that we needed to hire a chef, and by the time I had reached the parking lot, I was 100 percent certain. It was time for me to focus on other things.

    I contacted the culinary schools and placed an ad in our local paper. I needed a good chef. Inns of our size rarely had great chefs. My ad stressed the importance of a top school. There are a lot of chefs out there that just don't have a firm grasp of basic techniques. Ted was the first to apply, and we had a nice talk, but a few days later, he called and said that the commute from Vermont was too far. A few days later, Val applied. We sat on the front porch and had a very nice discussion. You could tell that Val really wanted this job and had spent considerable time envisioning this opportunity. While Val had not gone to a fancy culinary school, it was obvious the school of hard knocks had prepared him well. Val had a long and impressive résumé. Val was currently working as the chef for an assisted living center. They had told him that they wanted gourmet meals for their residents. In reality, the residents wanted everything overcooked, and Val hated the job and was even thinking that it was time for a career change. I emailed one of Val's references from a nearby inn. She simply said, "He is a good egg." Based on his enthusiasm, his correct understanding of how to make veal stock, and the reference, I hired Val Fortin.

Val grew up in Berlin, New Hampshire, under difficult circumstances. After high school, Val joined the Navy and saw the world. After the Navy, a caring uncle took him under his wing and introduced him to the culinary world. In the summer, they would work in the seasonal restaurants of New England and then migrated south for the winter. Val was an eager student, watching everything, taking good notes, and asking questions and reading cookbooks as if they were novels. It was also obvious that Val had natural culinary talent and was willing to work hard to develop it.

After meeting his wife, Nancy, Val settled down in the town of Lisbon, New Hampshire. Val and Nancy have been married sixteen years. Val has worked for most of the larger hospitality properties in the White Mountains, including the Mount Washington Hotel, the Bretton Arms, and Sunset Hill House. While working for the Mountain Washington, Val was part of an elite team that represented the hotel in international culinary competitions.

Val originally was going to start after the family's annual vacation to Maine. However, Val changed his mind about going to Maine and wanted to start as soon as possible. It was Labor Day weekend, and I had a lot of guests, so I was happy about an additional hand in the kitchen. I had already done most of the prep for the night, so I suggested that Val come in about 5:00 p.m. to be ready for the first table at 6:00 p.m. Val immediately took over, reducing my sauce to the right consistency and arranging everything for the night ahead. I watched Val execute the first few dinners with precision. I was no longer needed in the kitchen, so I joined my family that was visiting from New Jersey in the dining room. That was my last night in the kitchen, although I still am the breakfast chef.

Val was a self-starter and needed very little direction. We did talk a lot about our goals and vision for the restaurant, but I was not going to meddle in the area of menus and recipes or be a know-it-all about suggesting more salt or toning down the garlic. I really wanted Val to run the place as if it was called Fortin's. Slowly Val started to expand the menu with entrées such as duck and osso buco. Karen and I loved his duck so much we served it at our wedding. Other signature dishes such as the Trio of Soups and Val's Caesar Salad were early additions to the menu and have stood the test of time. I usually think of soup as a boring menu selection at a fine dining restaurant and usually ordered by those looking to shake off the chill of a cold night. Val with his Trio of Soups recreated this category. It was now all about flavor and an experience for the senses. Three espresso cups filled with a burst of flavor. I think that his white chocolate turnip soup is decadently delicious.

In the early days, there were things that stood out about Val and his food that are equally true eleven years later. The number one hallmark of Val's food is every plate is so visually delicious. The other very noticeable quality of Val's food is the layers of flavor. This is done through attention to the small details, such as finishing salts, truffle oil, a fried garlic chip, fresh herbs, freshly grated ginger, etc. Another notable characteristic is the strong sense of pride in being a chef and his reverence to the profession and its traditions and responsibilities. You can see it in his pride of wearing the uniform, belonging to industry associations, continuous study and experimentation, meticulously organizing the kitchen, and volunteering his time at culinary charity events. Val is a strong believer in hard work. Even in the slow season, when Val could have some extra time off, we see him in cleaning his ovens, rearranging his kitchen, and experimenting with new ideas.

Shortly after Val's arrival, I created a comment card for the restaurant. I think that guest feedback is very important, and to this day, we very carefully analyze every restaurant and inn comment card. It was originally a five-point scale ranging from poor to excellent. Then I modified it by adding a score of six for outstanding. It was my thinking that we would rarely achieve a six, but it would give us a target to shoot for. Based on our comment cards, we would consistently score either *excellent* or *outstanding*. Many guests were telling us that it was the best meal they ever had. What was interesting was that the most positive critiques were from our most traveled guests and those who went to fine dining restaurants the most. Of course, not everyone thought this. When it comes to food, personal preference varies a lot, and there will be a divergence of opinion for any restaurant no matter how good it is.

This positive feedback crystalized our thinking, and we set our sights on being the best fine dining restaurant in the White Mountains. The White Mountains are full of family restaurants, but there are very few truly top-end establishments. Val suggested that we set our sights on earning the Distinguished Restaurants of North America (DiRōNA)'s Achievement of Distinction in Dining award. The only DiRōNA restaurants in New Hampshire were the Bedford Village Inn and the Mount Washington Hotel. To become a DiRōNA restaurant required two years under the same management, a detail application that described every aspect of the restaurant operations, and a secret undercover inspection. Since it would be over a year before we could apply, that gave us the time to achieve the standard.

It's hard to be something that you haven't personally experienced, so we planned a series of field trips. While a grand tour of Europe's best restaurants would have been nice, it was not in the cards. Maybe someday. The first trip was an overnight stay and dinner at Manor Hoive in Canada. This is an amazing Relais & Châteaux property. The four of us had the tasting menu with paired wines. Every course was spectacular. For the cheese course, they had a cart with over thirty cheeses, and this young woman knew the name and details of every cheese. In my head, I was thinking, Where can you find such a person? This was the first and only time I spent $1,000 for dinner, but it was worth every cent. They also generously gave us a tour of the kitchen and all their inn rooms.

On another day, the entire serving staff (breakfast and dinner) attended a full-day workshop on serving techniques given by the

White Mountain Community College. This was where I learned to use a waiter's corkscrew. On another trip, we took all the dinner servers and kitchen help to dinner at Thorn Hill. They also gave us a tour that included rooms, kitchen, and wine cellar. Both the ownership and the chef have changed at Thorn Hill since that visit. We appreciated their willingness to share their years of experience with our team.

Another year, Val, Val's wife, Nancy, Karen, and I went to Quebec City and stayed at Auberge Saint-Antoine and had dinner at Panache. We analyzed everything we saw and tasted. I highly recommend St. Antoine. It is a wonderful boutique hotel. Our second night, we went to an innovative restaurant called Toast. It was on that trip that Karen and I became a couple. The old part of Quebec City is so romantic.

It's funny to say now that back in our first year, the dining room looked like a German beer hall. There was no hiding it even with white table clothes. At a meeting of the New England Inns and Resorts Association, we met the design firm of Truexcullins, and we hired them to give the dining room a completely new look. More about them in a later chapter.

When the time came, we sent in our application for DiRōNA. We nervously waited for the verdict. The inspector could be any one in the dining room, so every night we had to give it our best. About two months later, we received the good news in the mail. The report detailed everything, including calling for the reservation, how they were greeted when arriving at the restaurant, the service, and lots of details on the various courses. The report did indicate that our beverage service was not on the same level as the food. So we set our sights on earning the Wine Spectator award. Val and I went to Dallas to accept the award at DiRōNA's annual conference.

Chapter 12

The Dining Room

In 2006, if you wanted to give a generous assessment of the Sugar Hill Inn's dining room, you would see a delightful breakfast room. In the morning with windows on three sides, the room is bright and sunny. The room had natural wooden tables and simple schoolhouse chairs. The tables were topped with woven placemats, and the servers were wearing colorful *Little House on the Prairie* aprons. If the room could only speak, it would be inviting you for the best pancakes and sausage in town along with genuine local maple syrup and lots of hot coffee. The inn has always been known for its delicious breakfasts. If we were just a simple, old-fashioned B&B and not a full-service inn with big plans for the future, a little fresh paint would have been all that was needed.

However, my critical eyes were focused on two huge air conditioners cut into the wall. In the late sixties, I am sure that it was cool and reassuring technology, but by 2006, these dinosaurs were blowing only hot air. Also, the overpowering flowered wallpaper from the seventies was showing its age. Norman Rockwell prints were strategically hung to hide tears and holes in the wallpaper. There was also something about the design of the tables that made the room look like a German beer hall.

Carol, our interior decorator, was in charge of developing a plan to redo all our public rooms on the main floor. It was our thinking that first impressions count, and therefore, we would immediately focus on the rooms that everyone would see. Carol's expertise was in the area of residential design. Restaurant design was an entirely different ballpark. With so many projects underway, we decided that we would replace the worn wallpaper and redo the lighting. Carol selected very elegant wallpaper and Hubbardton Forge lighting. Having these fixtures throughout the main floor tied our common rooms together. Hubbardton Forge lighting is handmade of wrought iron in Vermont, and being local was important to us.

We also tried to hide the beer hall tables under tablecloths. While I dislike this saying, it totally applies to this situation. It was like putting lipstick on a pig. It would be another year for us in figuring out our next step.

In 2007, I was attending a meeting of the New England Inns and Resorts Association at the Mount Washington Hotel. The architecture and interior design firm of Truex Cullins had a table at the meeting displaying beautiful photos of their hospitality projects. A gorgeous cottage caught my attention. We were currently in the planning stage for the Dream Cottage, and I momentarily considered bringing them in on that project, but we were too far ahead with the planning, and that would have delayed the project.

Several months later at another meeting of New England Inns and Resorts Association at the Bethel Inn, Kim Deetjen, interior designer and principal of Truex Cullins, gave a thought-provoking presentation on green design. At the meeting, I told Kim about our dining room and inquired if this project would be something Truex Cullins would be interested in. Being relatively new to the restaurant business, I felt that we needed some expert help. How big should the tables be and how much space should be between tables? How do we create that elusive feeling called atmosphere? How do you decorate a traditional country inn dining room tastefully and stand out from the crowd at the same time? A few weeks later, Kim and her team of designers came to see the inn. Aside from measuring every square inch of the dining room, we also spoke about our goals for the inn and showed them our recently completed renovations, such as the tavern, library, and Dream Cottage.

In building the plan, there were three constraints. We would work with the current wallpaper and lighting since they were still very new, and the room design would be flexible enough to be reconfigured for special events such as weddings. Unlike most residential interior designers that make their money by buying at wholesale and selling at retail, Truex Cullins would receive an hourly rate for consulting, and the furniture would be at cost.

We received a very detailed plan via mail that included fabric samples, photos of furniture, layout drawing, and the design for a custom-built wine cabinet. An appointment was set up for us to visit their offices in Burlington to discuss the plan. Looking back on the plan, I have to give them a lot of credit for understanding both who we were and where we were going. They combined a traditional design with innovated ideas, sophistication, comfort, and fun. When you are paying a consulting fee, you are looking for outcomes that you could not have achieved on your own, and they delivered with great ideas.

Prior to our meeting, I was told that a newly hired employee would be coordinating our project. Val (executive chef), Nancy (Val's wife), Theresa (former assistant innkeeper), and I began our meeting by taking a tour of the facility. It was very impressive. They had catalogs from thousands of suppliers. There was nothing that they could not get. Following the tour, we sat down at a conference table with the designer appointed to coordinate the project. We began by just informally talking, but I assumed that she had a formal presentation for us that would logically take us though the plan. As someone who had worked years in the corporate world, I was ready for a PowerPoint. Instead, the meeting turned into an unorganized question-and-answer session. Although I loved the concepts and vision, I had concerns about the person they had put in charge.

The plan included a number of different seating options for our guests, including high-back chairs and love seats. All the tables had attractive wooden legs. They also designed a wine display that would be custom built for us. Not only would it display our growing selection of wine but would also hide the kitchen doors, and the backside would provide a work area for our servers complete with glass storage.

A beautiful handmade wool rug would show off a center table. The only thing that disappointed me about the plan was the recommendation for artwork. With so many cool galleries in Burlington, I was expecting something really interesting. At the end of the meeting, a few tweaks to the plan would be made, and then the purchase order would be sent over to me to be signed.

When what should have been the final plan arrived, I showed it to Theresa, the assistant manager at that time, for her input. She said that it looked crowded and was concerned that the servers would have trouble getting around the room. At first, I discounted her opinion; after all, Truex Cullins were hospitality experts. These details were the reason we hired them. Later we would learn that although they had built many very impressive hospitality projects, we overestimated their restaurant experience. Over the next week or so, I went out to eat several times. Everywhere I went, I would measure the table. I also fully set our tables with dishes and glassware to see how large of a table it would take for our style of fine dining. I reported back my thinking to Truex Cullins, and several new drawings were produced, but we were not getting anywhere. It was like being in a New York City taxi caught in traffic with the meter ticking. I complained to Kim, and she assigned a senior person to oversee the project and removed some of the nonproductive hours from the bill. Eventually all the details were worked out, and the paperwork was signed, and we waited for the big day when everything would be delivered.

The wine display arrived a few days ahead and was assembled on location. The craftsmanship was absolutely beautiful. We are still in love with that piece years later. The day the furniture came, Kim was on site to see that everything was perfectly placed. We set the room for dinner, and Kim made flower arrangements for each table. The room looked perfect.

Over the next few weeks, we did discover some things that we needed to adjust and some design quirks that we just needed to live with. We discovered that if we sat guests at the center table, the room was too crowded for the servers to maneuver, so we pulled the chairs from the table and used it display a fresh flower centerpiece. The location of a couple of tables had to be slightly adjusted because the center carpet runner impeded the free movement of their chairs. We also discovered that our high-back chairs did not work as well as we would have liked with the table bases, but this is something we have learned to live with.

On a trip to Quebec City back in 2008, Karen and I found the perfect painting for above the fireplace. This was the first expensive painting we purchased as a couple.

Overall, I would have to say that we have been very pleased with our dining room, and I can't think of any inn of our size with a nicer restaurant. Also years later, I can say that the design, fabrics, and furniture have all stood the test of time.

Chapter 13

Breakfast

To me, there is a big difference between a full-service country inn and a bed-and-breakfast, but many refer to both as a bed-and-breakfast. So if you are a bed-and-breakfast, it is extremely important that those two components, the bed and the breakfast, are taken very seriously, and we do.

One of the reasons for the popularity of the bed-and-breakfast is that a top-notch breakfast beautifully served creates a memorable experience in addition to tremendous value. To duplicate our breakfast at the famous pancake parlor up the road would cost over $40 per couple, and the same breakfast at a Boston or New York Hotel with tax and tip could easily be $60 to $70 or more.

At the inn, I wear many hats, and being breakfast chef is one of my jobs. Over the past ten years, I have probably made over thirty-five thousand breakfasts. During that time, I have intently focused on what people want. I have analyzed what people order, have listened to feedback, studied comment cards and reviews, and have stayed at other inns to see firsthand how others handle breakfast. The result of all this study is that there is no consensus, although I have identified some helpful insights.

My response has been to focus on choice. It has always surprised me on the number of inns, and I mean good inns, that don't offer a choice. There is no menu, and stuff just comes. They claim that they offer a selection by rotating daily between an egg entrée and a pancake-type dish. If you are there on an egg day and you don't like eggs, you are stuck. So why do they do that? It is the easy way out. They know their exact guest count, and they can mass-produce some egg dish. This is why so many inns serve baked eggs. The folks who arrive first will find it at the peak of perfection, and those who come near the end of breakfast will find their eggs to be overcooked and dry. To me, hospitality is doing what is best for the guest.

At the Sugar Hill Inn, guests arriving for breakfast are greeted by my wife, Karen, and are invited to sit anywhere they like. Everyone has their own table. I dislike properties where everyone is forced to sit at a communal table. Not everyone is in the mood to be social at 8:00 a.m. Karen offers coffee, tea, or cappuccinos. I like having cappuccinos on the menu because so few inns have them, and it reminds me of the hospitality I received while traveling in Italy. Cappuccinos are individually made, and it's our way of sharing the love of hospitality with guests.

In the real world, too few of us really have time to sit down and enjoy a leisurely breakfast. To those that drink their coffee from a paper cup at their desk or the parents that are rushing to get the kids out the door, we want to share the luxury of a leisurely served breakfast. The elegance of our dining room, combined with personal service, mountain views, and a multicourse breakfast is an integral part of the Sugar Hill Inn experience. I like tranquility in the morning. We once stayed at this very expensive bed-and-breakfast in Ashville, North Carolina, and the innkeeper was a Jay Leno wannabe and did a monologue that lasted throughout breakfast. It was so annoying we went elsewhere the next morning.

The bakery of the day is always served with coffee and honey butter. We whip New Hampshire honey into the butter. The bakery of the day is always homemade. Guests frequently ask for my raisin scone recipe. The next course is always fresh fruit. The fruit course is served while the entrée is being made. There is always a choice for the entrée between an egg-type dish and a pancake-type dish. For the eggs, it might be our famous crepe filled with scrambled eggs, ham and cheese, a French rolled omelet, or a scramble with sautéed vegetables and local cheese. For the pancake-type entrée, we frequently feature blueberry buttermilk pancakes, waffles topped with berries, ricotta lemon pancakes, or cream-cheese-and-strawberry-stuffed cinnamon raisin french toast. These entrées are served with apple wood-smoked bacon. Many people have asked us about where they can buy this bacon, but unfortunately, it is only available to restaurants. In keeping with our strong belief in choice, we also offer our homemade granola, English muffins with locally made jams and Special K with skim or almond milk and banana. Vegans especially like the English muffins.

It was my original intent to serve a very innovative and gourmet breakfast. I soon learned that was not what most of the guests wanted. Even those that were adventurist in the evening want traditional comfort food for breakfast. How do I know this? I would for example offer both an omelet with fresh crab and scrambled eggs with cheese, and the simple scrambled eggs would outnumber the more gourmet offerings by two to one. It surprised me that there was little interest in items like crab cakes or homemade gravlax. Some guests even find goat cheese to be scary. I have also given up on the whip cream on the french toast. As a chef, I loved to use whip cream because it makes the plate look so beautiful, but 90 percent of the guests were saying, "Hold the whip cream." It's important to listen. On a trip to Napa, I discovered this cookbook from a local and very expensive inn that served these decadent dessert, like breakfasts featuring dark chocolate in many of the recipes. I tried this one recipe where fresh fruit was presented in this chocolate cookie shell. Visually it was a sensation and tasted equally good; however, no one was fazed. Recently, Val has adapted the recipe for a dinner dessert with much better success.

Even though we were going to focus on traditional breakfast food, with an occasional deviation, I certainly needed to differentiate myself from the local diner. I do this by using the best local ingredients and creating visually appealing plates. Topping the eggs with local cheese, brightly colored sautéed vegetables, and fresh parsley not only taste better than plain old scrambled eggs but is visually delicious. Fresh fruit and a touch of powdered sugar on a pancake can do the same thing. The owner before me used a commercial pancake mix, but to me that is cheating. It is easy to make them totally from scratch, and you can taste the difference.

I also discovered that although guests want to indulge in items such as bacon that they don't regularly eat at home; they want to do it in moderation. We are often thanked for not overdoing the portion size. Our guests are generally active and fit and are looking to balance the pleasures of a great breakfast with plans for the day. However, if you are a big guy, don't worry, I am happy to send out your pancakes with a side of eggs and extra toast.

Guests are coming to the inn for an authentic New Hampshire experience, so we focus as much as possible on local products. Our eggs come from local farms. Farm-fresh eggs from cage-free hens just taste better. We also buy local maple syrup by the case. At $52 a gallon, it's expensive, but it's worth it. At a retail store, it can cost double what we pay. Our jams and jellies are made for us in Lancaster, New Hampshire. Even our coffee is roasted in New Hampshire. We place our order on Tuesday; it's roasted on Wednesday and delivered to us on Thursday. In the summer, we grow our own herbs and buy from local farms. We also served Harman's cheese, aged two years in Sugar Hill, and many other local cheeses. We have been Certified Local as part of the NH Farm to Restaurant Connection.

Another important principle is cooking everything to order. Many inns don't do this. Sure, it's more work, but it's worth it. Items like pancakes and eggs just are not meant to be made ahead and sit in a warming oven.

Special diets are becoming increasingly common, and we do our best to accommodate. We do ask if you do have special needs to let us know ahead of time so that we can buy the soy milk or eggbeaters that you require. Gluten-free is very common and easy to accommodate. We have gluten-free pancakes and waffles, and potatoes can be substituted for toast. Dairy-free is also common. For extreme diets, sometimes it is more helpful to know what one usually eats instead of everything they don't eat. Special diets can slow down the kitchen on a busy morning, so hopefully guests will use good judgment when making special requests.

We generally seat our guests between 8:00 and 9:00 am. On busy mornings, we extend the time to 9:30 a.m. It generally only takes about five minutes for me to produce entrées for a table of two. On most days, this works really well. Occasionally everyone arrives together, and then those five minutes can add up. On busy days, being well prepared is important. To be ready for a full house on a Sunday morning, I usually arrive by 6:00 a.m.

Our concept is not cast in stone, and I am sure that it will evolve as tastes and styles change.

Granola
- 3 cups rolled oats
- 1 cup slivered almonds
- 1 cup cashews
- 3/4 cup shredded sweet coconut
- 1/4 cup brown sugar
- 1/4 cup Sugar Hill maple syrup
- 1/4 cup vegetable oil
- 3/4 teaspoon salt
- ½ cup raisins

Preheat oven to 250.

Combine oats, nuts, coconut, and brown sugar. In a separate bowl, combine all wet ingredients and salt. Combine both mixtures and pour onto two sheet pans. Bake for one hour and fifteen minutes, stirring every fifteen minutes. Let cool and then add the raisins. Makes about six cups of granola.

Raisin Scones
- 2 cups flour
- 3 tablespoons sugar
- 1 tablespoon baking power
- 1/2 teaspoon salt
- 5 tablespoons unsalted butter, very cold, cut into cubes
- 1/2 cup raisins
- 1 cup heavy cream

Preheat oven to 425.

Add the dry ingredients into a food processor and pulse. Then add butter and pulse fifteen times. Add raisins and pulse again. Move the contents to a mixing bowl and add the cream. Mix with a spatula and then turn out onto parchment paper and lightly knead. Shape by pressing into nine-inch-ring from a spring-form pan. Unmold and cut into ten wedges. Bake twelve to fifteen minutes. Serve with strawberry butter.

Blueberry Sour Cream Muffins

- 12 tablespoons unsalted butter
- 1 1/2 cups sugar
- 3 large eggs
- 2 teaspoons vanilla extract
- 8 ounces sour cream
- 1/4 cup milk
- 2 1/2 cups all-purpose flour
- 2 teaspoons baking powder
- 1/2 teaspoon baking soda
- 1/2 teaspoon salt
- 2 cups New Hampshire fresh blueberries

Preheat the oven to 400 degrees. Place eighteen paper liners in sprayed muffin pans.

Cream the butter and sugar until light with an electric mixer. Slowly mix in the eggs, vanilla, sour cream, and milk. In a separate bowl, measure the flour, baking powder, baking soda, and salt. Add the flour mixture to the batter and hand mix while adding the blueberries a handful at a time. Scoop the batter into the prepared muffin pans and bake for twenty minutes, until the muffins are lightly browned on top and a cake tester comes out clean.

SECTION FOUR

The Good Life

Chapter 14

The Ten Reasons I Love What I Do

Even with the sixty-hour workweek, I enjoy being an innkeeper. It is the most demanding but best job I have ever had. Until buying the Sugar Hill Inn, I was never known as a workaholic. Being an innkeeper is more a lifestyle than a job. For those that can totally commit to the demands, I totally recommend it. It is the total confusion between work and play that is so seductive. These are the ten reasons I love what I do.

1. We have the best guests. I meet the most interesting people from around the world. A great conversation never feels like work. Guests pick bed-and-breakfasts and country inns because they value the personal connection not available at larger properties. There is nothing better than at teatime having total strangers share the tales of the day and travel tips. This is the only job that I know of where I can consistently please people 99.7 percent. Certainly even the best lawyer, teacher, doctor or financial planner cannot come close to those stats.
2. The inn is a happy place surrounded by natural beauty. We are a place for proposals, weddings, honeymoons,

vacations, adventures, romance, daydreaming, great conversation, fine food, relaxation, and luxury. There is always someone celebrating a birthday or anniversary.
3. I work with the greatest team of people. I enjoy their company and have the greatest respect for their talents and contributions to the inn.
4. I enjoy business, and it is very rewarding to see a "so-so" small business grow into something really special. It starts with a vision. A vision is just a really good daydream. The next step of strategy development is like a good chess game or playing sports. The final step of implementation brings the tangible rewards.
5. I am a professional student. I am always looking for something new to learn. To be a great innkeeper, there is so much to know. I am currently studying to pass the Certified Wine Specialist Exam. As I write this, I am also reading a book about Twitter marketing. My library is full of books on green construction and interior design. In the past year, I have read great books about the Ritz-Carlton, Four Season Hotels, and the Union Square Hospitality Group.
6. The Sugar Hill Inn is all about the fine art of good living. Where the simple pleasures of life are celebrated. A good wine in the right glass paired with great company, amazing views, and a leisurely environment adds up to much more than the sum of its parts. I always look forward to wine-tasting appointments with distributors. I send much of my free time searching art galleries and antique shops for the inn. I also get to dine at the best restaurant in the White Mountains most nights. No, I don't have all four courses. Is that fun, or is that work? Sometimes it is hard to know when you are passionate about what you do.
7. I get to live in an area surrounded by natural beauty. I just need to look up. Mountain Views are everywhere. I get to live all year round where guests, at most, can only enjoy it for a week. It is so refreshing to live in an area where you

do not need to worry about locking your car or house. We have no rush hour. Even on the hottest day of the year, the air is always fresh. Step away from the lights of the inn and we have the most fabulous sky of stars. From the wildflowers of early spring to the first snow of winter, every season unfolds with gifts of beauty.

8. Being the breakfast chef gives me a creative outlet. I enjoy working with good ingredients and making every dish taste as good as it looks. I strongly believe that food should be cooked to order, and I want my guest to enjoy the luxury of being served. Breakfast tends to be more about comfort food than being overly gourmet. When we are full, I enjoy the challenge of sending out the food as fast as the orders come in and seeing if the servers can keep up. Also at breakfast, if there is a low between orders, I visit guests in the dining room wearing my chef's coat. Sometimes we will talk about recipes and on other days about the best hikes to explore waterfalls and covered bridges.

9. I enjoy interior design and renovating. I can frequently be found in the design section of the Dartmouth bookstore. My ideas come from trying to uncover the essence of what it means to be a New England farmhouse, a county cottage, or mountain escape. It is not uncommon for me to lose sleep over an exciting idea. Seeing a room go from ordinary to extraordinary is very satisfying. As we renovate, I am constantly on the lookout for practical ways to make the inn greener. All newly renovated rooms are painted with zero VOC paint.

10. In the end, there are two factors that keep me going every day. The first one is celebrating our achievements. We have come so far so fast. This is not the same inn I purchased in 2006. The second factor is the challenge of knowing that there is so much more that needs to be done. The day I run out of ideas or lose the desire to take it to the next level is the day I sell out. I don't foresee that happening for a very long time.

Chapter 15

Karen's Story

I first met Karen in 2008, and she was also on a mission. I did not realize this until recently but both of us were seeking the perfect slice of New England life. However, we each had our own definitions.

The first thing that you will notice when meeting Karen is that she is very attractive and tall. The second thing that you will notice is her wonderful Southern accent. Don't be fooled by the accent. Karen has New Hampshire roots, unlike me. Her father was from Lincoln, New Hampshire. After graduating from Plymouth State University and serving in Korea, on the advice of his sister, he settled in Metro Atlanta and met Karen's mother. Every summer the family would travel north to visit Grammy in Lincoln, New Hampshire. Karen loved those trips and never wanted to go home.

In those days, Lincoln was a very different community. This was before skiing at Loon Mountain and before the interstate. Actually, Grammy's house was moved to make way for I-93. Lincoln was a close-knit small community. This was a family town. A paper mill was the largest employer, and everyone knew someone who worked there. The main street was store lined, and sidewalks connected the town. As a kid, Karen would ride her bike to the soft-serve ice cream shop and would order a cone with Jimmies. In the northeast, sprinkles are known as Jimmies. That was news to me. Karen also had fond memories of swimming holes, mountain hikes, lazy summer days, and the famous Clark's Bears.

It was always Karen's goal to move back to New Hampshire someday. With the responsibilities of everyday life, career, and raising three wonderful children, that goal was postponed but not forgotten. While Karen owned a very nice home in a quiet neighborhood of Marietta, Georgia, to get anywhere meant getting in the car and fighting traffic. It was time for a change. With the kids grown, the plan was back on. Karen was looking for the perfect New England town where she could find an older home around the corner from Main Street and walk to the library, church, and stores and meet friends for coffee.

Over the years, Lincoln had become much more touristy with a lot of development and maybe not enough careful planning. So Karen set her sights on Littleton. Littleton, just ten minutes north of Sugar Hill, has a great main street and a lot of character. A recent survey of America's best small towns ranked Littleton as number 6.

Karen is not one to procrastinate. On her very first day, she stopped in at the New Hampshire employment security office to get a list of job offerings. I can't say whether it was fate or luck, but the Sugar Hill Inn was on the list. We were looking for a part-time front desk person and help with the laundry. Karen said that she really needed full-time employment but could do anything that needed to be done. Front desk is the most important job at the inn because it involves all the important detail of running the inn and a lot of guest interaction. Karen was naturally good at the job. When I would overhear Karen on the phone, you would think that she had been trained by the Ritz-Carlton. At that time, Karen reported to Theresa, the assistant innkeeper, so I did not have that much direct involvement.

While I didn't know it at that time, Karen had given buying a bed-and-breakfast serious consideration. She toured both the Mullburn Inn and Horse and Hound when they were for sale. She particularly liked the Mullburn for its in-town location and that the home had originally belonged to the Woolworth family. This had extra significances in that Karen's parents had met at a Woolworth lunch counter. The bed-and-breakfast had an antique stove that was a gift from Thomas Edison.

At the end of the busy season, after fall foliage, Karen and I have different accounts of things, but basically the inn was very slow, there was little work available, and I was being very cautious due to the financial crisis the country was facing. In early spring, Theresa announced that she was leaving, and I quickly offered Karen the position of assistant innkeeper. Karen was visiting family in Georgia and started the following week.

With Karen's diversified career in tourism, property management, real estate, home furnishings sales, accounts payable/receivable plus her Martha Stewart homemaking skills of baking, gardening, sewing, entertaining, and decorating, she was the perfect replacement for Theresa.

Karen was a self-starter and jumped right into the position. I was pleased from the start. Sometimes I am too nice with vendors that are not doing their jobs as well as they should. I was impressed with her willingness to fight for the inn. I am sure that Karen would recount in that first year that I overly micromanaged and called her too frequently at home about things that could have waited for the next day.

One day Carol, our decorator, dropped off her bill, at the front desk, for redecorating the Moses Aldrich room. Karen could not resist commenting on the price. I explained that it included custom window treatment, bed skirt, and rug. We had just recently retiled the bathroom with beautiful natural stone travertine. Karen was right; if we were going to improve all fourteen rooms, we needed to make each dollar go further. Karen said that she could do it for less, and she was right. We had just renovated Wildflower, and the room needed curtains. This was Karen's opportunity to take charge. She brought me to a small workshop on a side street in Littleton. They had tons of books full of fabric samples. I have to say, looking at all those samples made me tired. It had exactly the opposite effect on Karen. Karen loves beautiful fabrics and could have spent all day in the shop. The curtains were ordered and were perfect for the room and did save some money by cutting out the middleman.

Up to this point, we worked well together, but we really knew nothing about each other. Back then, we did not serve on Thanksgiving, so I invited Karen to have dinner with my daughter, Sara, and me at the inn. At the last moment, Sara backed out, so we had dinner just the two of us. I guess you can say that it was our first date. I made the turkey, and Karen made the sides. We had a table for two in the inn's dining room in front of the fire. We shared a bottle of Tavel, a dry rose from the Rhône Valley in France. We each shared our life's story. I spoke about being a single dad, my parents, and my plans for the inn. Karen spoke about her two sons and daughter and why she had moved to New Hampshire. The dinner was most enjoyable. And while there were no sparks of romance, from that point on, we were friends.

As I explained in an earlier chapter, every year after our busy season, I would take the management team away to celebrate another season. Karen was now a part of the team, and we were on our way to Quebec City with our chef, Val, and his wife, Nancy. We had three rooms at the fabulous Auberge Saint-Antoine. It turned out that Karen and I were very good travel partners. We discovered that we liked doing the same things and enjoyed each other's company. Quebec is so romantic at some point we naturally held hands, and our relationship instantly changed. There was chemistry. We explored the city, enjoyed great food and wine, and purchased our first painting together. It was definitely apparent to Val and Nancy that something was up.

In running the inn, I like to think outside the box. Karen had a way of understanding what I was thinking and to encourage my ideas and to contribute with insightful feedback. Our hotel in Quebec had Nespresso espresso machines in all the rooms, and I was very impressed. For Christmas that year, Karen purchased a machine for me. Shortly after that, we added them to our suites, and today they are in all our rooms. We are the only lodging property in New Hampshire with them.

We clearly liked working together. Karen would come in early and help me prep for breakfast. On many projects, Karen would take the lead, such as expanding the parking lot, new outdoor lighting, and the design for renovating Bickford. If you ask Karen about her contribution to the inn, her answer would be modest. However, the truth is that Karen has extremely high standards, and the inn would not be what it is today without her. Innkeeping is a very demanding lifestyle with long hours. I truly appreciate the sacrifices Karen has made for the success of the inn.

To preserve our sanity, Tuesdays and Wednesdays are date nights. The restaurant is closed, and Elke will watch the front desk and wait for check-ins.

Even more than working together, we enjoyed traveling together. We had the most romantic trip to Napa and Sonoma. I remember sitting on the patio at Domaine Carneros, sipping champagne with a view of the vineyards. I introduced Karen to the world of fine wines and have discovered that she has an excellent pallet. On that trip, Karen added the Hess Select Cabernet Sauvignon to our wine list.

On a November 2012 trip to Charleston, South Carolina, I proposed to Karen. We were married at the Sugar Hill Inn the following April. We closed the inn and invited twenty-five of our closest family and friends. Guests started arriving on Monday. Various events were planned for the week, including lunch at the Mount Washington on Wednesday and dinner at Chang Thai on Thursday. The chef was given the choice of being a guest or being the chef. His answer was fast. "No one else is going to cook in my kitchen." The ceremony started at 6:00 p.m. followed by hors d'oeuvres and cocktails in the tavern. We then had a formal four-course dinner in the dining room. Karen and I selected our favorites from Val's repertoire, homemade ravioli for the first course, duck for the entrée, and Rivers Edge Pinot Noir from Oregon. Val's duck is the best. We had a three-piece band, and dancing went late into the night. It was truly a storybook wedding. On Sunday, we headed to the airport for our ten-day honeymoon to Italy.

Chapter 16

Original Art

If all you need is a decent place to stay while exploring Franconia Notch, I can recommend several well-run motels. However, if where you stay is just as important as or sometimes even more important than your daytime itinerary, the Sugar Hill Inn might be worth considering.

At the Sugar Hill Inn, we are all about sharing the good life with our guests and creating experiences that will be remembered. This means gourmet dining, stylish rooms, attentive service, and relaxing surrounding. As I write this, I am sitting at the pool, enjoying the sunshine, taking in views of Mt. Lafayette and listening to the soothing sounds of the waterfalls. It is important to surround our guests with beauty. Of course, that is not hard when almost every window has a mountain view. We also like bringing beauty inside, with stylish rooms, fresh flowers in the dining room, and original art.

So what is so special about original art? Don't all hotel rooms have art? Take a closer look and you will see that nothing is signed in most guest rooms. That means what you are seeing is just a copy. That same picture may be hanging in hundreds or even thousands of locations. Those prints might be decorative, but that is not art. The frames are worth more than the prints. There are websites with huge inventories that specialize in providing prints to hotels, offices, and hospitals. There are high quality printers that can print to canvas and produce results that look just like an acrylic or oil painting. In China, there are factories where workers copy the work of others. These workers are very skilled technicians, but they are not artists, and their work is not art.

While I can't explain the science, there is research that shows that original art contributes more positive energy to a room than a quality copy.

There are also numbered limited addition prints signed by the artist. While these are not originals, there is still a connection to the artist compared to larger unsigned print runs.

Now, I am not saying that every lodging property needs to have original art. If everyone did, it wouldn't be interesting. We do it because we enjoy being a collector, want to support local artists, and hope that our paintings will bring enjoyment to our guests. If a painting carries you away on a mini daydream, evokes an emotion, or contributes to a room's atmosphere, that's all that we can ask for.

Only recently we have started talking about original art as one of the core elements offered by the Sugar Hill Inn. While we have always loved beautiful art, in the early years we had to focus most of our effort on the fundamentals of innkeeping. Our interest in art for the inn has been an evolutionary process that has evolved over many years.

I have always been interested in art appreciation. Although I was an economics major in college, the art appreciation classes were always my favorite. When on vacation, I have always enjoyed visiting galleries; however, I was just a window shopper. The idea of spending over $1,000 for a painting, until recently, seemed like an extravagance that I could not justify.

When I purchased the inn in 2006, there was nothing of any value. Just cheap prints in cheap frames and lots of knickknacks from the QVC Country Hour.

I was fortunate to inherit several very nice paintings from my parents. They had good taste. They would frequently go to charity art auctions. A search of these artists on eBay shows that these artists still have a following, and their paintings have maintained or grown in value. It amazes me to think that these paintings that I grew up with are almost fifty years old, and they are as beautiful as ever. In that time, so many purchases, such as cars and TVs, have come and gone, but good art is forever. I hope that my daughter will keep these in the family.

About two weeks after buying the inn, Cynthia Knapton walked in carrying two framed limited addition prints and introduced herself as a local artist. She painted the fields of wildflowers that northern New Hampshire is famous for. She said, "I will leave these here on consignment." Since we had nothing else, we said fine. We thought she had forgotten them. A year later, she came back for her art. By then we had grown attached to them and offered to purchase them. Except for the art shows we have participated in, we no longer display art on consignment. I just don't like inns where everything has a price tag on it.

That first year, we also purchased a metal sculpture of a moose from the League of New Hampshire Craftsmen in Littleton. The moose still lives in our herb garden. League of New Hampshire Craftsmen has seven stores around the state and are certainly worth a visit.

I learned that Debbie Aldrich, one of our dinner servers, was a talented watercolor artist. We were in desperate need for something for the tavern, so we commissioned Debbie to paint our view. The painting was beautiful, but when we hung it in the tavern, it clashed with the wallpaper, so we moved it to the library, where it looked really good. It is now in the Bickford Suite, where it looks perfect. We have learned over the years that finding the perfect location is as important as finding the perfect picture. When the painting adds to the beauty of the room and the room enhances the painting, you have found the perfect location. My designer side calls it harmony, and the businessman in me calls it synergy. Since then, we have purchased two more of Debbie's paintings. We like that Debbie finds her inspiration right here in Sugar Hill.

WREN (Women's Rural Entrepreneurial Network) in Bethlehem operates the best local gallery. WREN is a nonprofit organization in northern New Hampshire that helps people start and grow businesses. They host a new gallery show every month of local artists. I generally stop in monthly to see what's new. At WREN, I discovered Larry Golden and Paula Wolcott. Two of Larry's paintings are in the Richardson Suite. Larry is a very talented instructor of art at the St. Johnsbury Academy. Paula is a resident of Sugar Hill, and her paintings can be found in the Perennial Room and tavern. The Sugar Hill Inn is a corporate sponsor of WREN because we would like to see the arts flourish not only at the inn but in the greater community.

I have also purchased art from sidewalk art shows in Sugar Hill, Littleton, and Lisbon. The sidewalk shows are fun because you get to meet the artist.

Up to this point, most of my purchases had been inexpensive and therefore relatively easy decisions. We certainly did not yet have a vision about making art an important part of the Sugar Hill Experience although we did like showcasing local artists.

In November 2010, my world was going to change. Every year after the fall season, I would take the management team on a trip to celebrate the end of our busy season and to experience hospitality at its best. That year we went to Quebec City. Although the Le Chateau Frontenac is the most famous hotel in the city, we stayed at St. Antone, in my opinion, the best hotel in the city. Karen was now the assistant innkeeper, so naturally she was invited along with Chef Val and his wife, Nancy. At this point, our relationship was strictly business. The second night, we had a fabulous dinner at Panache, the hotel's restaurant, followed by ice wine in the lounge. After all that sitting, food, and drink, I needed some fresh air before going upstairs to bed. So I explored the quaint cobblestone streets near the hotel. While nothing was open, all the shop windows were lit. I discovered this amazing painting of wine bottles. I made a mental note that I must come back tomorrow when the gallery would be open.

The next day, the four of us toured the city. By about 4:00 p.m., Val and Nancy had had enough of sightseeing, so we dropped them back at the hotel, and I invited Karen to go with me to see the painting I had seen the night before. The gallery had several paintings by Nathalie Chiasson, all with wine themes. The wine theme resonated with us because we had recently made a strategic decision to increase our wine list from 45 bottles to over 120 bottles and earn the Wine Spectator Award of Excellence. I loved the painting that I had seen in the window the best. Karen also loved the painting. I really wanted to buy the painting, but if I had been there myself, I am not sure I would have. I had never purchased a painting of that quality before, but with Karen's support and encouragement, I did. It was an exciting moment. We were telling the salesperson all about our inn and how this painting would be perfect for our dining room. You could feel the electricity in the air. I think also in that moment, we became a couple. That night, the four of us dined at another great restaurant called Toast. That night following dinner, I did not walk alone. The streets of Old Quebec at night are extremely romantic.

We are frequently complimented on the painting and asked about the subject matter and the technique. The wines are all very well-known Super Tuscans. Her technique involves multiple layers of paint and glaze. Her secret ingredient is coffee.

For those of you saying that Quebec is not local, let me remind you that we are only seventy-five miles from the Canadian Border.

In 2012, when planning the renovations for both Garden and Forest View, the idea about art as a component of the Sugar Hill Inn experience came into maturity. For these rooms, the art was not going to be an afterthought. Now art was going to be in integral part of the planning processes. We even planned for the proper lighting. Lighting is so important for displaying art. For inspiration, we spent time in Portland, Maine, and Quebec exploring the galleries and shops. In Quebec City, we did find two paintings that did inspire us, but we needed to pull all the components of the room plans together first.

When it came time to order the painting for Forest View, we learned that it had already sold, but the artist would be willing to have us commission something similar. We would be under no obligation to buy it if we did not like it. Being a commission, we were able to request more blue in the palette and the addition of a mountain in the background so that it would look like New Hampshire. Karen was in charge of the design for Garden, and although she had already found a painting she loved, it was the wrong dimensions for above the bed. The commission process worked so well for Forest View we decided to try it again. This time we were disappointed. To our eyes, there was an area that looked like dripping paint, and we felt that it would be easy for the artist to correct. However, the artist was insulted and felt that his work was perfect and would not consider any adjustment. So we purchased the original painting we had seen and placed it across from the bed instead of over it.

By late 2012, we were totally committed to making original art a core element of the Sugar Hill Inn experience, but collecting art takes time, and we didn't want to prematurely emphasize it until we had reached critical mass. On a trip to Montreal in November of 2013, Karen and I found a painting by Michael Rozenvain that grabbed my attention. It was colorful, full of movement and detail. When buying art from a gallery, there is never a reason to feel rushed. Galleries are happy to e-mail you all the details for consideration. Because of the high taxes in Canada and the lack of sales tax in New Hampshire, it generally makes sense to have a painting shipped. I was still thinking about the painting in December, and we really needed another spectacular painting for the inn's common areas. Once again, my comfort zone was being tested. I understood that this was a very complex painting that could only be painted by a very accomplished artist. With Karen's support and encouragement, we purchased the painting that is now in the tavern. We have been very happy with the painting and the positive comments of our guests.

So where do we go from here? Since we enjoy art collecting, it will be an ongoing endeavor. Now that I have overcome my fear of spending money on art, I will try to constrain myself to one big purchase a year. Some of our earlier purchases may be retired to make room for higher quality art. We are very pleased with the positive feedback from our guests. It is also our goal of trying to encourage the arts within our community.

Chapter 17

Bartending

I was never really one who hangs out in bars. It never really made sense to me to be standing four deep at the trendy bar of the moment or waiting in line at the cool club, hoping to get in. The sports bar with the huge flat screen TVs and cheap beer was also not my style. If I had the remote control, we would have been watching CNN or the TV Food Network.

However, I have always liked hotel bars. Those in the top hotels always seem so classy and comfortable whether you are seated in a comfy leather club chair, at a cozy table for two, in front of a massive hand-carved mahogany bar, or on an outdoor deck with mountain views. The quality of the service, drinks, glassware, and inviting atmosphere makes a huge difference to me. I know that you pay a premium for this, but to me, it's worth it. On a recent trip with Karen to Washington, DC, to visit my daughter, Sara, we enjoyed resting our tired feet after a day of sightseeing at the Willard Hotel Bar. I am a sucker for the salty treats, and vodka tonics can be so refreshing. I also love the outdoor European cafés. There is nothing better than sitting in the square of an Italian hill town with a glass of local wine, taking in the views and people watching. Packing a bottle of something in my suit case and drinking it from the bathroom cups to me seems very unappealing just to save a couple of bucks. By the way, at the Sugar Hill Inn, we are always happy to send you back to your room with Riedel stemware.

Hotel bars don't need to be large, but they do need to be inviting. It was our plan to have such a bar at the Sugar Hill Inn. We refer to the room as the tavern. We have noticed that guests that spend time in the tavern enjoy their stay more than guests who don't. Even if you don't drink, enjoy early morning coffee, afternoon small bites, or the new tavern dinner menu. The tavern is the heart of the inn. Being a small, intimate inn, you don't need to be very outgoing to strike up a conversation with another guest or staff member. It's interesting that at a large hotel, there is almost no interaction between guests, but at a small inn with only fourteen rooms, it is easy and natural. This is why staying at a small hotel or inn is so inviting, and stopping for a drink in the tavern before dinner is so worth it. Do you want the inside scoop about what to see and do, just hang around the tavern.

My knowledge of bartending was very limited when I purchased the inn, and what I did know I learned mostly from my family. My family always drank vodka tonics. The lime was very important. When my brother married Barbara, the family was introduced to gin. My grandfather's drink was a highball. To him, this meant Canadian Club and ginger ale. After the first sip, he would say, "The good Lord knows I need it." From my parents' travels, I learned about Campari and Grapa. My dad did a lot of business in Switzerland, and after dinner, they would smoke these funny hand-rolled cigars and drink Grapa. My mother was a light drinker but did enjoy champagne. She also liked to add Kirschwasser along with sugar to fresh strawberries for dessert. From my brother and his underage friends, I learned about the 7and 7. Fortunately, he is all grown up now and likes Belvedere on the rocks. For my daughter's high school graduation party, I found the perfect recipe for frozen margaritas. These were for the adults only, and they were delicious. My daughter is twenty-nine now and likes bourbon. I am sure that her liking bourbon dates back to me being politically incorrect by saying women generally do not like the stuff.

Obviously in that first year, I did not have the skills to be my own bartender, so we hired Deb. Over the years, Deb had acquired bartending skills at several jobs. At that time, I was not in a position to analyze her bartending knowledge, but her personality seemed perfect for the job. We went on a shopping trip to the state liquor store, and I purchased whatever Deb said. Deb's skill as a bartender was basic, but guests loved her because she always had a story to tell. If we were running behind in the dining room, Deb would tell one of her bear stories, and no one would want to be seated until the end. She was also good at introducing guests and encouraging conversation. Many people who met her before dinner would go back after dinner just to pick up the conversation they had previously started. At the end of the season, Deb announced that she would be going to Florida to help her daughter, who was expecting her first baby.

Next we hired Susan, and she was equally good but very different from Deb. Susan had just completed the program at the Boston Bartending School, and to her, bartending was a serious profession. She was a doctor of the cocktail. Guests would tell her their likes and dislikes, and she would make a customized drink. Susan also developed price lists, systems, and procedures so that the bar could be a serious profit center. Susan also taught the staff, including myself, the fundamental of bartending so that we could manage on her day off. Bartenders depend on tips. Being only a small inn puts a cap on how successful any bartender could be, so at the end of the 2007 winter season, Susan took a position with the Mount Washington Hotel. We have stayed friends with Susan and Deb, and from time to time, they would pop in for a visit.

After Susan, I became the bartender. It was true that both Deb and Susan could outsell me; however, the incremental sales were less than the added payroll cost. It also gave me more direct contact with our guests, which was both good for me and our guests. Pour someone a couple of drinks and they will tell you anything you might want to know.

In the planning stages for the tavern, I would have dinner at the bar of the better local restaurants and observed what was on display, their equipment, and the drinks that were being made, and how they were made. I have also learned a ton from just listening to my guests. I have to say to my more extroverted friends and colleagues that listening is highly underrated. One day a guest called to make a dinner reservation and said it was her husband's birthday, and she wanted to know if we had Basil Hayden's Bourbon, her husband's favorite drink. I said I was not familiar with it, but if it was for sale in the state, we would get it. When the couple arrived at the table, a glass of Basil Hayden's on the rocks was waiting as requested. That night, we added the bottle to our Bourbon shelf, and it has become very popular. I learned early that the premium brand of my parents' generation and my early adulthood was now considered ordinary. Smirnoff has been replaced by Grey Goose, Belvedere, Ketel One, Ciroc. Jim Bean and Jack Daniel's have been replaced by Nob Creek, Maker's Mark, and Basil Hayden's.

We have the nicest guests, and one day someone gave me a bottle of Talisker ten-year-old scotch. Thinking that I did not like scotch, I put it on the shelf, and to my amazement, it started to sell. I had no idea how special that bottle was. For years, people would drink blended scotch such as Chivas Regal, Dewar's, J&B, and Johnnie Walker. A blended scotch is a mix of both malt whiskies and grain whiskies, sourced from several different distilleries. By doing this, the producer can create a flavor profile with mass appeal and a consistent product from year to year. Blends represent 90 percent of scotch sales, but not at the Sugar Hill Inn. The excitement in the marketplace is all about single malts. Each single-malt scotch is very distinctive. These are very popular with our guests. Tasting and collecting single-malt scotch among enthusiasts and connoisseurs is a growing trend.

Premium small batch bourbons are also very much in fashion. I recommend Whistle Pig from Vermont. It is 100 percent straight rye whiskey although not technically a bourbon.

At the bar, the more demanding a patron is, the easier it is to please them. A serious drinker knows exactly what they want and will clearly spell out exactly how their drink should be made. We also have many guests who at home rarely drink and don't really know what they want. In many cases, there is a vague memory of a drink enjoyed years ago on the honeymoon in Barbados. Also, I think the guests were hesitant to ask for things we might not have. To fix this problem, I developed a drink menu. Creating this menu was a major step in upgrading our beverage service. Being a small bar, we had to pick carefully what to stock. My goal was to develop a list with wide appeal. We included many of the classics that are back in style, such as Old Fashions, Tom Collins, and Manhattans. The drink menu not only helped the undecided but also played an important part in raising the bar for our beverage service.

As with most undertakings at the inn, it is a two-step process. At first, the goal is to become competent and comfortable followed by taking it to the next level of perfection. Each drink was researched to develop the perfect recipe. We now measure precisely the ingredients for each drink. This method makes a perfect drink every time. The recipes are on index cards, so anyone on the staff could pour a drink if I was not available. Careful measurement is not considered amateurish but instead the preferred method of serious bartenders. The free-pour method, based on a count, is popular at busy bars because it is faster. We also banned all mixes such as Bloody Marys or margarita mixes. For a good margarita, all you need is good tequila, Cointreau, fresh lime juice, and simple syrup. The mixes are way too sweet. For those who like their Bloody Marys spicy, I go back to the kitchen and request freshly grated horse radish.

I remember when having a premium beer meant drinking an import such as Heineken. While I still have Heineken and Stella Artois, we sell very few. Remember when lite beers were big? They are dead in the water too. The big nationwide brands such as Budweiser also don't sell well at the Sugar Hill Inn. It's all about local micro brews. This is great for us because we want guests to experience our local New Hampshire beers. We frequently recommend that our guest visit our local brewpubs for lunch or a causal dinner. The other trend is cult beers, and a glass of these beers can be as expensive as a glass of wine. We sell Dogfish Head 90 Minute Imperial IPA for $10 a glass. I thank my younger staff for keeping me informed on these.

A well-made drink in a nice glass, relaxing surroundings, and the company of your special someone is all part of the good life, and that is what the Sugar Hill Inn is all about.

Chapter 18

Wine Adventures

As innkeepers of an upscale inn, it is our job to share the good life with our guests. In a small way, we get to share in that lifestyle of great food, fine wine, and beautiful and luxurious surroundings.

In April of 2015, we were staying four nights at Hotel La Cep in Beaune, France. This hotel, in the heart of Burgundy, is the preferred place to stay for wine buyers from around the world. We had two prearranged wine tastings. Wineries give restaurateurs the royal treatment. Our first meeting was at Maison Louis Jadot. Louis Jadot is the largest exporter of Burgundy wines in the world. The facility was ten minutes out of town in a new and very attractive space. First, we were taken to the fermentation room, where they explained their approach to wine. In some ways, Burgundy is simple to understand. The reds are Pinot Noir, and the whites are Chardonnay. However, the French believe in the concept of terroir. The soil and microclimate makes wine from every village in Burgundy unique. Even two vineyards within a single village can be very different. Louis Jadot owns vineyards throughout Burgundy and also buys grapes from other growers. It is their goal in making wine to interfere as little as possible so that each wine is an expression of its terroir.

Our next stop was the barrel room, where we tasted fourteen wines straight from the barrel. A special tool called a wine thief is used. They wanted us to taste the small nuance of each village. At past tastings, I always ignored the fact that professional wine tasters spit instead of swallow. However, it was 10:00 a.m., we had fourteen wines to taste, and I had to drive us back to our hotel in a foreign country with a stick shift car. So I tasted like a professional and did not swallow.

After returning to town, having a quick café lunch, our next appointment was at Maison Joseph Drouhin. Here we had a wonderful guide who told us that his grandfather was in the French resistance during World War II. Joseph Drouhin's wine cellars date back a thousand years and extend under the historic town of Beaune. Once again, we tasted about fourteen wines. Since we could walk back to our hotel after this tasting, I did not need to be as careful.

The next day we explored the villages, driving past some of the most famous vineyards in the world—Romanée Conti, Pommard, Volnay, Meursault, Clos de Vougeot, Montrachet. This is the holy land for wine lovers. However, ten years ago, none of these names would have meant anything to me. In my past life, I always avoided French wines because I did not understand them. I have come a long way.

I have always enjoyed wine, but before buying the inn, my knowledge was average at best. At the French Culinary Institute, they had a very brief unit about wine as part of the chef program. We learned the difference between a Cabernet Sauvignon, Merlot, and Pinot Noir but not much more.

Orlo, the former owner, suggested that I contact Ken Scupp. Ken was a high-level executive at Kobrands, a huge distributor and importer of wine. While developing wine lists was not part of his job description, he really enjoyed helping new restaurateurs learn about wine. Ken wrote, priced, and printed the list containing about thirty-five wines. Most, of course, were from the Kobrand wine portfolio, but they were all good picks with wide appeal. The thing about selling the same wines night after night is after a while, you really get to know what you are selling. We would frequently change the wines by the glass so that the staff would have a chance to learn and taste. Our small list gave us the feeling of certainty in the huge and overwhelming world of wine.

In November 2006, we had our first wine dinner. The thinking was, having an event in early November would expand the fall season and give people a reason to stay with us when business normally slows down. Val wrote the menu, and Ken paired a wine to each course. Between courses, Ken would introduce the wine selection. The dinner was a big success, and the event became an annual tradition. After the first year, we decided that every year would have a theme, and we moved the date to March. So far we have done France, Italy, Spain, Napa and Sonoma, New Zealand, Argentina, and Germany. In 2015, we did France for the second time, and in 2016 did Italy again.

In preparing the promotional material for the first dinner, I learned that Ken was a Certified Specialist of Wine. From a web search, I learned the designation was from the Society of Wine Educators. All I needed to do was to join the associate, study their wine manual, and take a one-hour exam, and I too could be a Certified Specialist of Wine. The manual was so full of detail it was unreadable. It was also full of foreign terms. While I can sound out a Spanish or Italian term, the French terms are not pronounced anything like the way they are spelled. So I started self-study with books like the *Windows on the World Wine Course* that was written so that the average person could understand it. Thinking that a deadline would be helpful, I registered for the examination three months down the road. Time flew by and I was not really ready but sat for the exam anyway. I missed passing by just a few points. The pass rate is only 50 percent of test takers. Being so close, I reregistered again for the exam. With additional time to study, I was so much better prepared. Once again, I missed passing by just a few points. It was obvious that they had made the exam more difficult.

For many working in the industry, becoming certified helps them with their career path. Being an innkeeper, this is certainly not a requirement. Someday when I do have the CSW designation, I will most likely be the only innkeeper who is a Certified Specialist of Wine. For now, I am going to let my knowledge of wine grow by everyday involvement in the industry, talking with guests, reading, an occasional day of study, and travel. When I am ready, I will take the exam again and pass.

As I have stated earlier in the book, I am a professional student that is always interested in learning new stuff. Wine is one of the most fascinating subjects to study because it includes history, religion, culture, traditions, science, geography, business, travel, food, and more.

Learning wine also is about developing your senses. What do you see, taste, feel, and smell? The back of the bottle or a wine review might talk about cherries or vanilla; however, to the beginner, details might be hard to identify. Developing the senses can't be rushed. One day while enjoying a glass of wine, it will hit you. "Vanilla. Wow! I get it." Now from your studying, you will put two and two together. Vanilla comes from aging wine in new oak barrels.

There is research that shows that wine improves the enjoyment of food. It's not the alcohol, because a cocktail does not seem to have the same effect. Wine can take any meal and make it special. When Karen and I cook at home, opening up a bottle of wine can make even the simplest meal special. Wine has a way of slowing down a meal and encouraging great conversation. I see it in our restaurant; wine drinkers enjoy their dining experience more than the "Just water, please" or "Give me a Bud" crowd.

In 2009, we earned the DiRōNA Award for dining for the first time. To qualify, a secret inspector dined and evaluated our restaurant, and we received a very detailed report about all facets of our operations. One of the conclusions was that we had outgrown our simple wine list, and our beverage service was not equal to the rest of the dining experience. So I set the goal of earning the Wine Spectator Award.

How good is good. Selecting the industry's standard of excellence as our goal forced us to up our game. There are three levels to Wine Spectator Award—Award of Excellence, Best of Award of Excellence, and the Grand Award. We have the Award of Excellence. The minimum requirement is 90 wines; however we have about 120. For an inn of our size, that is a serious undertaking. Most of our competitors have not qualified. In fact, in New Hampshire, only eleven restaurants have earned the award. The Bretton Arms and the Manor on Golden Pond are the only other inns on the list. Neither of whom we consider to be direct competitors. On Tuesdays and Wednesdays, we frequently dine out. It surprises me how limited the wine lists are at the other local restaurants.

To earn the award, every restaurant must apply annually. The application includes a one-page description of your wine philosophy and concept. They are very interested to know how you are storing the wine. You must also submit a copy of your wine list and menu. We used an independent consultant to develop our first wining list although I was very involved in the process. Although many wine reps would love to help you, they are biased to the line they represent. Our list is large enough to cover all the international varietals and major wine-producing countries at various price points. Have you ever been to a restaurant where the list is so long that you have to make a choice to ignore your partner or read the list? Those are the restaurants where a good sommelier can be very helpful.

There is an important lesson that every restaurateur must learn. Just because I had never purchased expensive wine in my past life does not mean that there aren't people who can afford, enjoy, and want them. Although our average wine sale is $40 per bottle, we would be leaving money on the table if we did not also sell wine in the $60 to $150 range. We do have some wines over $150, but that is a very small portion of our overall sales. Research shows that most people gravitate toward the middle of the list. Having expensive wines on this list helps to boost the average selling price.

We actively seek feedback from our guests, and two issues arise from time to time. Why don't we have more wine by the glass, and why do we charge so much for them? A wine bottle once open has a relatively short life. Being a low-volume restaurant, if we had too many wines available by the glass, wine would be wasted or served past its prime. Neither would be a good thing. However, we usually have all the major international varietals covered. For whites, that includes Chardonnay, Sauvignon Blanc, Pinot Grigio/Pinot Gris, and Riesling. For reds, we usually have Cabernet Sauvignon, Merlot, Malbec, Pinot Noir, and Red Zinfandel. We also have French champagne, Prosecco, and an American sparkling wine by the glass. The sparkling wine is available as splits, the perfect one-glass serving. So why do some restaurant charge $6 or $8 a glass when we charge $10 to $15 per glass? They do it by serving cheap supermarket wine with big markups. Whether we are selling wine by the bottle or by the glass, we sell only wines that we believe to be quality.

My father-in-law looking for lively dinner conversation would frequently pose the question, "Are expensive wines better then cheap ones? I can't tell the difference. Maybe its just all marketing." Since my father-in-law enjoyed playing the devil's advocate, you never really knew his real position. Since he was not one to buy expensive wine, I think what he was really asking is a $10 supermarket wine much different from a $15 bottle. The answer is both yes and no. As I became more involved in the industry, I would be invited to trade functions where I would be exposed to excellent wine, and I can say now that there is clearly a difference. But that is not to say that an educated consumer can't find an occasional great deal or overpay for something rather ordinary. In a good restaurant, the sommelier should be helping you to find those hidden selections of superior quality and value that will pair perfectly with your dinner. I encourage guests to ask questions about our wines. There are so many wines available in today's marketplace there are going to be a lot of unfamiliar labels.

The producers of Vino Nobile Di Montepulciano invited Karen and me to a wonderful tasting for the trade in Boston. We even met the Mayor of Montepulciano. After a short presentation, it was time for a serious tasting and buffet dinner. There were about twenty different wineries, each offering several different wines to taste. We really enjoyed these wines. Karen and I composed a list of our favorites with the intention of adding one of these to our wine list. As a restaurant licensed in New Hampshire, we can only sell wine approved for sale in the state. At that time, only one of the almost one hundred wines featured at this tasting was available to us. So we added it to our list with excellent result. We have the same issue when we read a great wine review in the trade press only to find that it is not available in New Hampshire. We also attended a similar event for the trade sponsored by the Portuguese Wine Producers.

The best way to learn wine is by travel. In the spring of 2011, Karen and I planned a trip to Napa and Sonoma. Ken Scupp arranged for several VIP tastings. We also stayed at several wonderful Select Registry inns. Our first stop was Domaine Carneros. Carneros, just north of San Francisco Bay, because of its cool climate, is perfect for Pinot Noirs and sparkling wines. The famous French Champagne house of Tatingers owns Domaine Carneros. In keeping with their pedigree, they designed their winery to look like an elegant French Chateau. We sat on the front patio, overlooking vineyard, sampling champagnes and Pinot Noirs paired with tasty treats. I remember learning that pink champagne pairs well with barbecue.

Our next stop was Benziger in Sonoma. A member of the Benziger family gave us a personal tour of the vineyard and explained the importance to them of biodynamics viticulture. Biodynamic viticulture is a philosophy combining the maintenance of sustainable soil fertility and the recognition of the link between plant growth and the rhythms of the cosmos.

In Napa, we visited Cakebread. Cakebread is known for extremely high quality and expensive wine. We have a few of their wines on our list, but because of their high price, they are slow sellers. There is a buzz in our kitchen when a really expensive bottle is sold. We have a 2007 Cakebread Celler, Dancing Bear Ranch, Howell Mountain at $182. This is our most expensive wine on the list. If I can't sell it, I am going to have a fabulous retirement party someday. To protect their reputation, they are careful to sell only to upscale restaurants. The winery is beautiful. It looked more like a boutique hotel then a factory. We had a private tour of the facility, ending up at a conference room overlooking the production floor. We sampled wine, talked about our restaurant, and learned a ton about wine. It surprised me to learn that their grapes were all handpicked. This winery visit along with the others was arranged by Ken Scupp. Kobrands in New York has a whole department that arranges VIP winery visits for their customers.

Wineries are everywhere in Napa. Some are the big names that everyone knows, like St. Francis, and other are small boutique producers that rarely sell wine out of state. Because land values are so high that Napa focuses primarily on premium wine. The cheap California wines are from the central valley.

Our next appointment was at Sequoia Grove. A chocolate and Cabernet Sauvignon paired tasting had been arranged. Our host poured us a glass to sip while touring the vineyard and winery. At the end of the tour, we were brought to a large conference room with a large board table. At one end of the table were two placemats. On each placemat were three glasses of Cabernet Sauvignon paired with fabulous chocolate. Our host said "Enjoy" and left us to experience the chocolate and wine in privacy and undisturbed. It was romantic, delicious, and decadent all at the same time. If cooking a romantic dinner at home, I would highly recommend pairing a great cab with equally great chocolate.

Needing a break from wine, we decided to tour the art museum at Hess. On the way out, I could not resist taking a quick look in the tasting room. Since we did not have a prearranged tasting here, they wanted to sell us a tasting. I said I was not interested because we had already had two tastings so far today. I explained how I owned a restaurant and asked, "If I only have room for one of your wines on my list, what would you recommend?" He poured us each a sample. Karen absolutely loved the wine and decided that we must add the Hess Collection, Mount Veeder, Napa Valley to our list.

Upon returning to New Hampshire, we learned that Distinguished Restaurants of North America was going to be holding its annual meeting in Napa in the spring. Believing that being exposed to the food and wine culture of Northern California would be inspiring for the chef, we invited Chef Val and his wife, Nancy, to join us for this return visit to California.

Belonging to DiRōNA is a real privilege for the Sugar Hill Inn. Most of the member restaurants are not only larger but many of them are famous with celebrity chefs. Whether it is called an annual meeting, trade show, or conference, I have been to more than my share. While most come with PowerPoint presentations, and this was no exception, this meeting was all about food and wine. The first day, we had a growers' luncheon at the Napa campus of the CIA (Culinary Institute of America). We started with a tour. Very impressive kitchens. The Napa Valley Grape Growers Association sponsored the lunch. The food was marvelous, but it was really all about the wine. Every producer was coming by the table to pour his or her best. You would have a half-glass of one wine and then pour it out to try another. Reflecting back on it, we were drinking wines that on a restaurant's list would be between $75 and $200 per bottle.

On another day, we went to a workshop at Silver Oak about aged wine, led by the winemakers from Cakebread, Silver Oak, Chateau Montelena, and others. Chateau Montelena was one of the winners of the Judgment of Paris. All the wineries participating in this workshop were the best of the best. These were wines that were generally only in the hand of collectors. Most wines are not made to age. Unless a wine is perfectly balanced to start with, time will only magnify its flaws. These wines were magnificent. The other highlights of the meeting were the lunch at Francis Coppola Winery and the reception in the Beringer wine cellar.

On the last day of our honeymoon, in Italy, we stopped in the beautiful hill town of Orvieto for lunch. We sat in the piazza across from the most amazing cathedral, circa 1330, enjoying homemade pasta and drinking the refreshing local white wine. I can recreate that special moment at home by cooking a favorite pasta and by opening a bottle of Orvieto. That is the magic of wine. The inn's wine list includes a Ruffino Orvieto Classico along with our other favorites from Italy.

I hope that this chapter might inspire others to explore the world of wine. However, I certainly don't want to give the wrong impression that the enjoyment or even caring about wine is a prerequisite to enjoying a stay at the Sugar Hill Inn. The point is, we took one element of hospitality where we were weak and focused on it until we were strong and enjoyed the process. Over our ten years, we have repeated this approach over and over in building the business.

Chapter 19

Going Local

If we can grow it in our garden or make it in our kitchen, that's ideal. Buying cheese, maple syrup, eggs, produce, and art from Sugar Hill makes us happy. When not available in Sugar Hill, we seek out made in New Hampshire followed by New England.

Some people just need a place to sleep while visiting the White Mountains. That is not the business we are in. We are here for guests that believe where they stay is an essential part of the overall experience. Providing an authentic Sugar Hill/New Hampshire/New England experience is important to us. You will not get that at the Hampton Inn. You will also not get it at properties that heavily discount on Priceline, Travel Zoo, or Groupon. The details we worry about are the first to be cut by discounters.

For eleven years, I have been making Sunday morning crepes filled the eggs and ham for breakfast. The original recipe came from a well-known French bistro in New York City. Although they always tasted delicious, at first, nobody was ordering them. So I replaced the Gruyére cheese with Harman's Cheddar from Sugar Hill, supermarket eggs with local cage-free eggs, Polish Ham with North Country Smoked Ham, and a national brand flour with flour from the Littleton Grist Mill. Today our famous Sunday morning crepes are extremely popular.

We think of local in broader terms than just food. Unlike many in the industry, we do not bring foreign workers in on Visas. We think that it is important that your breakfast server is a local. When my decorator recommended Hubbardton Forge light fixtures, handmade in Vermont, for all of the inn's common areas, as opposed to made in China, I knew that she understood. My wife, Karen, sewed many of the window treatments, bedspreads, decorative pillows, and bed skirts. Karen is in love with fabrics, colors, and texture. Take a look in on Bickford or Garden; that is her workmanship.

Going local is nothing new. That is the way it has been for most of history. Anyone who has been to Europe knows how great those local farmer's markets are. They are in every town. In the fifties and sixties with the growth of corporate agriculture, huge consumer products companies like Kraft, and more women returning to the workforce, food became a commodity, beautifully packaged, frequently frozen, sold in large supermarkets, and designed for a fast supper. Most family-friendly chain restaurants are just selling fancy TV dinners.

In 1971, the year I graduated from high school, Alice Waters opened Chez Panisse, a Berkeley, California, restaurant that became famous for its organic, locally grown ingredients and for pioneering California cuisine. How ironic that in 2006, my first year in New Hampshire, I would be reading her biography while dining alone at an Applebee's. I highly recommend the book. Alice would make it a point to visit local farmers to see what they were growing. At that time, she had no idea that she would be starting a movement.

Another book that I highly recommend is *Animal, Vegetable Miracle* by Barbara Kingsolver. In that book, a family agrees to eat only locally for a year. While a great read, the idea is too radical for me. For me, it is important to put the wants and needs of my guests first. Of course, they want real maple syrup from New Hampshire, but they also want orange juice from Florida, strawberries when they are out of season, whiskey from Scotland, and wines from France, Italy, and New Zealand. So, our approach has been to add local elements wherever possible but not to deny anyone their favorite luxuries from around the world.

Occasionally we need to back off on a local product. We found this extra thick and extra meaty smoked bacon from the North Country Smoke House. Great flavor! For some reason, our guests have a thing for crispy bacon, and lean, thick-cut bacon does not get crisp. From time to time, we do buy some of their other products that are all superb. We had also for several years experimented with locally made soaps.

I am not trying to prove a point or be elitist. I am just trying to do what feels right. I remember being in my local bakery before moving to New Hampshire and seeing a truck pull up, and in came several trays of their special gourmet cookies. What kind of bakery doesn't bake their own cookies? I was so disappointed. Call me naive, but I was totally surprised when at Shaw's deli department, I saw those pretty salads being refilled from a box. Obviously, there are no elves in the back room.

Whenever I dine out and the dessert menu appears, I always ask if the desserts are made in house. Ninety percent of the time, the answer is no. If they come from a fabulous kitchen down the street, that's fine; however, most of the time, they are purchased from a large food distributor, made in faraway factories using ingredients that you would never use in your home kitchen. That explains why almost every restaurant seems to have a Mississippi mud pie. At the Sugar Hill Inn, all desserts are made in house, including ice cream.

Being local is as simple as celebrating the seasons. Being excited about the first local strawberry or the first ripe tomato picked from the inn's vegetable garden. I have childhood memories of eating the best corn on the cob grown by my grandfather and cooked immediately after being picked. The natural sugar in corn as soon as it is picked starts to convert to starch. That is why I would never buy supermarket corn.

Shortly after buying the inn, Nancy and Lon, the former owners of Sunset Hill, invited me to have dinner in their private residence. At this dinner, I had fiddleheads for the first time. Fiddleheads are actually young fern fronds that have not yet opened up. Fiddleheads grow wild in the North Country and are only available for a few weeks in June. We also have wild chanterelle mushrooms growing in the White Mountains. The combination of being unique to the area and seasonal is local at its best. Every summer, Lars, our mushroom hunter and expert, will show up with a box of chanterelles with a handwritten bill on a scrap of cardboard. At the end of the season, he will disappear until next year. I have no idea what he does the rest of the year.

Going local means different things to different people. Some are environmentalists worrying about all the unnecessary greenhouse gasses caused by shipping food to distance markets. While that is not my motivation, I see little logic in importing Evian water from France.

I have already said that my number one reason for pursuing local is to create an authentic New Hampshire experience. Number two is quality. Nothing can beat a tomato just picked from the garden or an apple from a nearby orchard. Between June and September, we buy the most amazing strawberries from Four Corners farm in Vermont. They are generally twice the price of supermarket berries, but they are worth it. In the fall, we keep a bowl of Windy Ridge apples out for the taking. These are the kinds of foods that create memories. We serve local eggs, and guests can clearly tell the difference. Why is there such a big difference? Supermarket eggs can be weeks old compared to just a few days. Cage-free and premium feeds also make a difference. However, if you are a hard-boiled fan, it is my understanding that old eggs work best.

Going local supports our local economy, and that is a good thing. In the process, I have met some impressive businesspeople, and they are a pleasure to work with. These are fellow entrepreneurs that I can relate to. Dan of White Mountain Canning comes to mind. His jams, jellies, and honeys have freshness you can't find elsewhere.

I know that coffee beans, with the exception of Hawaii, don't even come from anywhere in the USA, but a brand that at least identified with the region was a step in the right direction. When I purchased the inn, the previous owners were buying from New England Coffee, a Massachusetts company. Every other week, Ruth would call us to see what we needed; however, if we had not paid the prior invoice fast enough, a doe doe in accounts receivables would cancel the order without notice. My experience with accounts receivables people is that they do more harm the good for their employer. We dropped New England Coffee for Green Mountain Coffee, a Vermont company. We liked that they sold Fair Trade Organic Coffee. In 2006, Green Mountain purchased Keurig. With the tremendous success of the K cup, Green Mountain became a hot stock on Wall Street, and the company lost interest in serving local businesses and outsourced the job to a distributor. They also stopped making the hospitality packs that we used in our rooms. Convert your rooms to K-cup or else. We were now forced to buy from a distributor who had no affinity for coffee, and we were just an account number. As I frequently do, I wrote the president of Green Mountain to complain about their lack of customer service. I am still waiting for an answer.

After doing tastings from several local roasters, we selected White Mountain Gourmet Coffee. It takes knowledge and talent to be in the coffee business. There is a lot more to it than just being local and a nice guy. Every Tuesday, Richard, the owner, calls us for our order. The coffee is roasted on Wednesday and delivered on Thursday. Going local with our coffee not only gave us better quality but also gave us better service and supports the local economy. Unlike New England and Green Mountain Coffee, White Mountain Coffee treats us like a valued customer, and they are just fine with us paying with one check for all deliveries at the end of the month. A lot of big companies do not understand that trust is a two-way street, and a handshake is more powerful than a contract and arbitrary policies.

Visitors come to New Hampshire for our beautiful mountains, rural landscape, and quaint villages and towns. By supporting our local farmers, we are helping to maintain the state's rural character. Guests of the Sugar Hill Inn are also doing their part by preserving a historic 1789 farmhouse, fourteen acres of natural woodlands, and a business that can trace its roots back almost ninety years.

Getting started with going local is harder than it sounds. Unlike states like California, New Hampshire has a relatively short growing season. New Hampshire, unlike its neighbor Vermont, with its counterculture, was late to the artisan food movement. In the nearby town of Bethlehem, every season there seems to be a new farm-to-table restaurant. Unfortunately, they close at the end of the season, never to return.

The problem is that everything is more expensive, and you need to be in it for the long haul. It takes time to educate your guests as to the value of local, to demonstrate its superior quality, and the time it takes to be discovered. It is a serious commitment.

In the early years, I planted blueberry bushes, served local syrup, used flour from the Littleton Grist Mill, but all that really did not add up to that much. It took five years for the blueberry bushes to mature and to produce a significant amount of fruit. Three factors played a significant role in moving us from "nice try" to being "Certified Local" by the State of New Hampshire.

Chef Val, his wife, Nancy, Karen and I attended a meeting sponsored by the New Hampshire Restaurant Association. We heard presentations by other restaurants about their success with farm to table, we met vendors from New Hampshire, and we received a handout of the requirements to be certified local. This handout became our road map. In the car, I asked if everyone was on board. Everyone agreed.

This road map assigned points to every category of food. Some things we were already doing, such as featuring local beer. Other items took some research. We needed to replace the Poland Springs bottled water we were placing in our rooms with New Hampshire water. Not only were we successful, we found out that we could have it delivered by our beer distributor at a lower cost than we were previously paying at the supermarket.

For milk and dairy, it was as easy as identifying the local brands. Why buy Philadelphia cream cheese or Breakstone sour cream when you could buy Cabot. We learned that Cabot was a cooperative of New England farmers, including New Hampshire. Stony Field Farm's organic yogurt that we serve at breakfast is also made in New Hampshire.

Finding made in New Hampshire became a fun adventure. We needed five New Hampshire wines. Most of the in-state wineries were using grapes purchased out of state or making wine from other fruits. Neither scenario was of interest. We discovered that Candia Winery grew their own grapes, but we wanted to see for ourselves. Karen and

I followed the GPS to a suburban development twenty minutes east of Manchester. We found a ranch house with vines in the front yard. A sign from the driveway pointed to the back door for the tasting room. We went down five steps to the basement. There really was not a tasting room, but at the bottom of the stairs, we met the owner and tasted several wines. Behind him were some small tanks obviously used in the wine production. This was a one-man show. He grew the grapes, made the wine, and did the marketing. Most of the varietals were unfamiliar to me. They had been cultivated to withstand New Hampshire's cold climate. The wines were all sweet. You can hide a lot of imperfections when sweet. They also had a line of what they called ice wines. In premium ice wines from Canada, the grapes are handpicked from frozen grapes still on the vine, producing not only a sweet wine but wonderfully intense flavor. The New Hampshire ice wines are made by freezing the grapes after harvest. I call that cheating. Figuring that these were the best we could find in New Hampshire, we purchased a few cases and headed back to the inn.

In addition to wine, we have General Stark Vodka. General Stark was New Hampshire's revolutionary war hero who coined the saying "Live free or die." At the request of one of our frequent guests from Maine, we have Cold River Vodka. We also have Whistle Pig, a straight Rye from Vermont.

As part of the certification process, Charlie Burke, the volunteer leader of the Farm-to-Restaurant program, met Val, Karen, and me at the inn and reviewed our paperwork. More importantly, he was a wealth of knowledge as to local farms and vendors. Just recently, he recommended a New Hampshire farm for lamb. This lamb, currently on the menu, from Meadow View Farm in Gilmanton, New Hampshire, is absolutely the best.

Our research uncovered a wealth of local cheeses. As a result, we added a local cheese course to the menu that could be enjoyed instead of dessert or as an additional course. This might sound funny to people from big cities, but frequently at these local creameries and farm stands, you help yourself and leave your money in an unattended box.

Another important factor in helping us go local was the opening of the Littleton Food Coop. We own four shares. They have made it a point to feature as many local items as possible. This has been most helpful because many farmers don't have the ability or interest in small retail sales.

I am the breakfast chef, so making progress in the morning was relatively easy. However, I also needed Chef Val to be totally committed. Going to the DiRōNA conference in Napa did the trick. Aside from sampling mass quantities of great wine, world famous chefs were giving presentations about growing their own produce and herbs and the relationship they had created with local farmers. All this was very inspiring, and Val came back with ideas and plans take the restaurant to the next level.

Going local is a never-ending search for what is next. The green beans that were abundant and perfect last week are no longer available, but for the next two months, we will be able to source seafood from a New Hampshire–based fleet of fishing boats. I know that many of our guests are quite aware and appreciate our efforts. For everyone else, I hope that on a subconscious level, our quest for getting the details right is contributing to the overall feelings of enjoyment and well-being.

# SECTION FIVE

Business

Chapter 20

Core Values

I have always had a vision in my head of what the Sugar Hill Inn could be. I have been fortunate to have a dedicated team of managers and employees who have understood that vision, and through their talents, we have achieved so much. I believe that we have reached the point in our development where formalizing these values in writing will help keep us focused. I also believe that sharing these ideas with the public will help us find those guests who share our vision.

The Sugar Hill Inn is much more than a beautiful inn with fourteen attractive guest rooms with scenic views. It is the staff of the inn working together and united by a common set of core values that creates the Sugar Hill Inn experience. In 2006, I found a diamond in the rough, and every day we polish the discovery. Our goal is to create the perfect romantic mountain getaway.

We understand that our guests in the real world are active and busy and often don't always have time to enjoy all of life's simple pleasures to the fullest. At the Sugar Hill Inn, we want to make those pleasures numerous and easy. For some, it might be our local farm apples, for others, that we are the only lodging property in New Hampshire to have espresso machines in the rooms, or having just the right single-malt scotch.

Quality defines us. While others in our industry are cutting corners to offer discounts, we are focused on quality. For us, quality equals value. Quality is rarely a single issue but instead the careful execution of numerous details day in and day out. We understand that your time away is a precious resource, and everything must be perfect. Being a romantic getaway, we like to focus on plush robes, soft sheets, comfy beds, and sensuous milk chocolates. Quality is also about the things you don't see, like good maintenance and housekeeping. We buy the best beds, sheets, and towels we can find. As a Select Registry Inn, DiRōNA Restaurant, and AAA-listed property, we are subject to surprise inspection. We welcome the scrutiny, and our quiet competitiveness drives us to set our sights and then achieve top-level awards in the field of hospitality (Distinguished Restaurants of North America Achievement of Distinction in Dining, Wine Spectator Award of Excellence, Best of New Hampshire, *Yankee Magazine* Editor's Choice, and Open Table's Dinner Choice Award).

There is no other profession where you can make people happy 99.8 percent of the time. We are people pleasers by nature. Unlike a big city hotel with formal airs, I like to think of it as real people serving real people. It is our policy to hire our help locally, provide year-round employment, and treat our staff as family. Listening is the key to good customer service. We carefully read all feedback. More importantly, we encourage our guests to speak up while visiting us. We have solutions for most issues whether large or small. Need extra muffins for your hike, your room is too hot or too cold, or your pillow is too soft? Our staff is well trained and we have instant solutions for most problems.

We celebrate our geography, history, and New England traditions. We love our town and encourage everyone to explore the back roads of Sugar Hill. The White Mountains with its mountain peaks, waterfall, and covered bridges is heaven on earth. We proudly support our local artists and farmers and, when possible, buy products made in New England. Our farmhouse dates back to 1789 (the same year George Washington was elected the first president of the United States), when it was the Oakes farm. The Richardson family in the 1920s added a large addition and converted the property to a country inn. We take our responsibility seriously to preserve the property for future generations.

No stay at the Sugar Hill Inn is complete without dining with us. We strongly believe in the romance and lost art of fine dining. We have a European philosophy about dining. The table is yours for the evening. Take your time to enjoy the candlelight and cozy fire with the combination of great food, wine, and conversation. Our four-course menu offers a well-balanced symphony of flavors and leads guests through a leisurely, romantic, and artistic culinary experience. We are very fortunate to have Val Fortin as our executive chef. Val takes the time to do it right and is always thinking about how to take it to the next level. Everything is made from scratch, using local ingredients when available.

We love art and the artists who enrich our lives with their creativity. Since buying our inn in 2006, we have been building a collection of original works of art. This is not the fastest way to fill the walls of our inn, but we would rather take the time to find original works of art than to display mass-produced prints from a hospitality catalog. Original art brings the concentrated energy and creativity of the artist into the room, enhancing the guest experience. While our collection includes art from all over the Northeast, we take particular pride in exhibiting artists from Sugar Hill and our neighboring towns.

As innkeepers, we are the set designers of memories. Country inns are popular because they all have their own unique personality compared to the big-box hotels. Our character was not created in a design studio but instead comes directly from our history, location, and passions. It is our job to create those special places that encourage relaxation and romance. Every room at the inn is a unique offering, and we encourage guests to study the website before booking, to find just the right room that speaks to their sense of style, comfort, and value. We believe in good design and beautiful spaces. We love beautiful fabrics, tiles, and natural woods. Our style is understated luxury with an emphasis on comfort. It is important to us that our decorating selections be true and compatible with our historic farmhouse. We believe that maintaining beautiful grounds and gardens is also about creating special spaces for our guests. The pool was positioned to capture inspiring views of Mt. Lafayette, and the waterfall spreads tranquility to the entire backyard. In future years, we plan to increase our emphasis on landscaping. Over the last ten years, our renovations have touched all fourteen rooms. We understand that keeping a historic inn fresh and beautiful is a never-ending commitment.

At the Sugar Hill Inn, we do not claim to be perfect, but we are very proud that we get better every year. We achieve this by working together as a team, listening to our guests, learning new skills, investing in our facilities, and staying true to our core values.

Chapter 21

Business and the Community

I have spent about half of my career as an employee and the other half as a small business entrepreneur. In this chapter, I am really addressing those that have never owned their own business. I would like to clear up some common misconceptions about business, the struggle to keep government happy, the insurance monster, and the value of a business to its community.

As someone who has worked hard to achieve, I am sensitive to an undertone of negativity toward business. I know that most of that is aimed at big business. To the surprise of many, a big business is just a small business that has grown wildly beyond the expectation of the founder. People like Steve Jobs, Jeff Bezos, Elon Musk, Mark Zuckerberg, Larry Page, and Sergey Brin are my heroes. Yes, they have become very rich, but they have also created millions of jobs, advanced our living standards, and have contributed tons of tax and charitable dollars for the good of everyone else. In some ways, these individuals have shaped our world in more profound ways than anyone in Washington. Unfortunately, few businesses achieve this kind of success.

Many small businesses fail, resulting in serious financial pain for the owners. There is no minimum wage for entrepreneurs to guarantee a living wage. Business is all about risk taking. Play it safe, copy what everyone else is doing, and maybe with good management, you will eke out a living. Thinking outside the box will result in greater success or a bigger flop.

Most people go into business for themselves, because they have a craft or trade that they enjoy doing or they have new ideas that they wish to develop and introduce to the marketplace. Others go into business because they want to control their own destiny or seek the freedom of being their own boss. The freedom that entrepreneurs seek tends to be elusive. When you are the boss, you are never truly off or carefree.

Before you can practice your trade or explore your passion, there are fees and paperwork that need to be done first. And I just don't mean taxes. The following must be renewed every year for the inn involving paperwork, time, and fees—liquor license, food service license, corporate registration, trade name, boiler inspection, etc. Our water must be tested four times a year by the state. False positives can result in even more testing, forms, and fees. Every time we hire a new employee, there is paperwork. Forget to check box 3D and your paperwork will be mailed back.

In all fairness, I have to say that our local town of Sugar Hill is well run and a pleasure to do business with. As a former resident of New Jersey, I can say that it is certainly easier to do business in New Hampshire.

As a businessperson, the last thing that I want is for an employee or guest to be injured at the inn. However, sometimes I think the regulators have lost sight of their mission and are more focused on forms and fees. They also have no idea of the impact and cost that a new regulation may have. Unlike big businesses who have whole departments devoted to compliance, small businesses must fend for itself. Although I do my best to stay informed, I am sure that there are laws being passed in Concord and Washington pertinent to the inn that I am totally ignorant of. One of the more confusing things is payroll. There are too many land mines here to take chances. That is why almost any company with more than a few employees uses a payroll service.

I am neither an expert on insurance or building codes, but this is how it looks from my vantage point. Property insurance along with workers comp and auto insurance is one of our larger expenses and is absolutely necessary and required. Occasionally we get the question of why we are so pricy. The answer is that there are so many expenses that have absolutely nothing to do with our core mission of hospitality.

For years, our commercial property insurance was not that much different than having home owners insurance although much more expensive. You paid the premium each month, and they left you along. We have never filed a claim and have a perfect safety record. About three years ago, our insurance company contacted an independent insurance inspection company to visit their properties. They are paid to find issues, and that is what they did. Many of their suggestions were reasonable, and we quickly complied.

When it comes to safety and fire protection, there is always room for better technology. Regulators are continually updating building codes as better methods become available. If I were constructing a new building, not only would I be required to follow the best building practices, that is of course what I would want to do. The question is, with an older building, do we replace perfectly good and effective system every time building codes change? Our local town officials are very familiar with the inn and are guided by good common sense. I can't say the same for the insurance companies we have worked with.

Two years ago, our insurance company had us replace a perfectly good fire suppression system for our restaurant kitchen with the then latest and greatest. We also did everything else they asked, and the next year they came back with a new set of demands. While poorer, we are not safer. It is this collusion of big government and big insurance that is needlessly hurting small businesses and driving up costs. This year we will be changing companies, but I am sure that we will continue to experience similar issues in the future. In the long run, these costs are passed along to consumers. In a similar way the unintended consequesnces of the Dodd Frank Wall Street Reform and Consumer Protection Act is hurting community banks and main street businesses.

I am most proud of our contribution to our community. We employ a staff of twelve and support our local stores, farmers, venders, plumbers, painters, electricians, artists, etc. We also refer our guests to the local attractions, stores, and restaurants. Anyone who has studied economics knows that there is a multiplier effect as these transactions makes their way through the local economy.

We also contribute $20,000 in property taxes to the town of Sugar Hill, most of it going toward education. Since we do not use the schools, this is a net contribution to our community. I am a believer in good schools, so I am not complaining, but I mention it because I want my readers to understand how a business contributes to the community and also to have a better idea of the underlying costs of being in business.

The State of New Hampshire has a 9 percent meals and rooms tax. We collect over $55,000 per year for our state government. Although technically it is our guests who pay the tax, the cost of collecting it (credit card fees, filing requirement) fall on us. I think that most travelers look at the total cost of travel so that the larger the bite of government, the less there is for the private economy. Fortunately in New Hampshire, taxes related to hotels and dining are about half of that charged in many big cities such as New York or Boston.

It seems like a week doesn't go by without receiving a request by a local organization for a donation. We give gift certificates to numerous organizations and enjoy being generous and supporting our community. Since we can't give to everyone, I recommend to fund-raisers, patronize those businesses you call on. Every other year we give Public TV the ultimate weekend away in the Dream Cottage, including dining and a hot stone treatment for their annual auction. I understand that the cynic among us will say we are just being self-serving. I like to think of it as win-win. I see it with tipping at the inn, generous givers are the happiest people.

Every year we participate in the Taste of the Nation Manchester to raise critical funds needed to support Share Our Strength's efforts to end childhood hunger in New Hampshire and across the nation.

We are also active in Respitality, a program offering a night away to parents with special needs or ill children.

I have been an active member of the Franconia Notch Chamber of Commerce. Serving Six years on the board of directors. While it is true that most people join because they believe that it will help their business, unfortunately, there are many businesses that are freeloaders. They benefit from the increased tourism in the area without paying membership dues. To avoid embarrassment, I will not name names. For those that volunteer their time to be president and to chair committees, I salute you and thank you for making our community a better place to live and work. We also belong to the Western White Mountain and Littleton chamber.

If you ask someone about his or her hometown, they might start off with a memory of their school days, friends from the neighborhood, and move on to their favorite stores, restaurants, and landmarks. The restaurant where special occasions were celebrated with the grandparents or the coffee shop where you would meet your friends. Discovering that your favorite diner has been replaced by an office building or the drive-in theater is now a shopping center is bound to create a sense of sadness.

For many, the Sugar Hill Inn is that iconic business. We are their favorite neighborhood restaurant or their special romantic getaway. While Karen and I are the sole legal owners, so many of our guests and local residents consider the Sugar Hill Inn to be their place. After almost ninety years of operations, it would be impossible to count the number of birthdays, anniversaries, engagements, honeymoons celebrated at the Sugar Hill Inn. I meet people from time to time that fondly recall that they had their first summer job at the inn. Even people that have never stopped in but drive by occasionally would feel a loss if one day they discover their scenic landmark has been replaced by a condo development. Times change, and businesses come and go. The Sugar Hill Inn, over its long history, has had owners with the vision to keep the inn relevant and vibrant.

Running a small business might not be the easiest way to earn a living, but the priceless rewards of providing a living to a great team, preserving a historic landmark, creating thousands of happy memories, and being an important member of the community makes it worthwhile.

Chapter 22

Being the Best in the World

Back in the late seventies, I was in the MBA program at the College of William and Mary. We had great discussions about companies like GE, who made grand pronouncements about not being in any market where they would not be number one or two in market share. Fast-forward to today, I read a lot of business books. I want to know what today's best minds in the world of business are thinking. My favorite author is Jim Collins. His books include *Good to Great*, *Great by Choice*, *Built to Last*, and *How the Mighty Fall*. What makes these books so good is that they are backed up by rigorous research. I would strongly recommend these to both the entrepreneur and corporate employee. Recently while reading *The Everything Store* by Brad Stone, I learned that Jeff Bezos of Amazon had also been influenced by the concepts in *Good to Great*.

As I was reading *Good to Great*, I came across a concept that at first seemed impossible. This is not an exact quote, but he was basically saying, you need to be in a business/market where you have the potential of being the best in the world. I pondered this issue for days. With thousands of hospitality properties worldwide, how could I ever be the best?

To a lot of people, the best in the world refers to those places in exotic locations and are popular with celebrities and are certainly out-of-range price wise to most travelers. These places are frequently written up in travel magazines and find their way on to those top ten lists. However, if I have no plans ever to travel to Dubai or Bora Bora and can't afford a $1,000 per night, those hotels, while interesting to read about and it's fun to marvel at the photographs, are irrelevant.

In my travels, I rarely stay at the same place twice. However, there are a few places that I never tire of, and they are my best in the world. For example, Karen and I love Auberge Saint-Antoine in Quebec City. Quebec City is less than five hours from Sugar Hill and is a beautiful city with cobblestone streets, art galleries, and great restaurants. The hotel is centrally located in the lower town and has very stylish rooms, a great bar, fabulous bathrooms, and Panache, the best restaurant in the city. While the hotel is not inexpensive, it is still affordable. This is also where Karen and I fell in love and truly became a couple. To us, this is our best in the world. No Priceline deal is going to get me to stay elsewhere when in Quebec. I know that we have guests at Sugar Hill Inn who have the same connection to us as we have to Saint-Antoine.

It did not take long for me to conclude that Zermatt Switzerland and Sugar Hill, New Hampshire, were two very different worlds, and not every property was my competitor. We don't cater to tour groups, families, and the budget traveler. If a guest was specifically looking to stay in Franconia Notch, I have very little serious competition, and we are talking about a very small world. For others, the criteria might be a place within a three-hour drive of Boston or a seven-hour drive from New York. If I defined my world as New England, this would still be a daunting task to be the best.

Fortunately, the world has changed, and there are numerous niche markets that are too small for big business. Have you ever seen a fourteen-room Ritz-Carlton? Of course not. Their corporate overhead and management system is way too cumbersome for such a small property. Remember the good all days when we all watched the same three TV channels, listened to top forty radio stations, drank a handful of nationally advertised beers, and Holiday Inn was running ads that proclaimed, "The best surprise is no surprise." The world has changed. People want products and services that cater to their very individualist tastes and desires. There are hundreds of TV channels, dozens of micro brews in every state, and thousands of songs that can be instantly downloaded from iTunes. And yes, we do want to be surprised in positive ways. We want Amazon not only to find us the best-sellers but also the books that appeal to our unique interests. This phenomenon is described in Chris Anderson's book *The Long Tail: Why the Future of Business Is Selling Less of More*. This is truly the golden age of small business. So what does all this mean? Being the Best in the World is very personal and in the eye of the beholder.

When I purchased the inn in 2006, I identified the inns that I deemed to be my competitors. They each had long traditions of excellence. Maybe in their niche they are the best in the world. Given the run-down nature of the Sugar Hill Inn back then, I doubted that I was even on their radar. It would only be logical for me to copy what these more successful inns were doing. However, a copy is only a copy, and a copy could never be the best in the world. I needed to find my own path.

Seth Godin's books, especially *Purple Cow*, have also influenced me. Seth Godin also talks about the need to be the best in the world. He describes how on a trip to the French countryside, at first, all the cows were so interesting, but after a while, all those farms with cows were becoming boring. "If only there was a purple cow, that would be interesting." The point is simple; to be the best, you need to stand out.

Some in the business world may think that this is nothing more than the age-old marketing concept of differentiation, but it is different. Differentiation is a marketing technique to make similar products like Crest and Colgate or American and United Airways seem unique when in fact there is almost no difference.

Although there have always been inns, and they are certainly different than hotels and motels, too many of them have fallen into the sameness trap. These Victorian Inns appeal to an aging population, have overpowering wallpaper, too many knickknacks, look like Grandma's house, and serve afternoon tea. Being different is not about being strange or weird. Nor is it a marketing gimmick.

It was my goal to rethink the hospitality concept and make it relevant to the next generation of inn goers. While we would keep many of the best traditions of the past, so much really needed to be rethought. My thinking was very much influenced by the emerging boutique hotel movement. In the months leading up to the takeover of the inn, I was busy writing the website. This process was like going to therapy, hard and slow. We were not describing what currently existed but instead a new vision.

Some may think that I have some nerve for even talking about the topic of being the best in the world. I want to make it clear that I am a very modest person and would never claim that we were the best in the world. And by Jim Collin's criteria, we have not met the test of time. On the other hand, I see tremendous opportunity to rethink hospitality and, within a small niche, strive toward excellence.

In some ways, my task was easy when compared to a three-hundred-room hotel. I have only fourteen rooms to fill, so I could focus on being the best in a small niche. A larger hotel, in order to fill all those rooms, needs to appeal to the lowest common denominator. That is why even at the upscale chains such as Marriot, the rooms are bland and functional.

At the Sugar Hill Inn, I know that 99 percent of my guests are leisure travelers, and most of them have romance on the agenda. Our guests seek an experience, not just a place to stay. We also don't take children, no room sleeps more than two, and we have only one bed per room. Because we have purposely limited our target audience, we can focus just on the needs and wants of this narrow group and be very good at it. We have made our website extremely detailed not only to attract those finding our offering to be compelling but to discourage those that do not share our ideas about hospitality.

Our focus at the Sugar Hill Inn is on being a romantic getaway known for fine dining and stylish room, and in that context, I will highlight some of the ways we have chosen to stand out from the crowd in this chapter. The broad topics of romance, stylish guest rooms, and dining are discussed elsewhere in the book.

Almost every health club has a sauna in both the women and men's locker room. Why? Because many people enjoy them. It is the ultimate luxury, and that is why our Dream Cottage has a sauna. Imagine after a great day of skiing warming up with your partner in your private in-room sauna. Guests love it, and it's only available at the Sugar Hill Inn.

Have you been to the Museum of Modern Art in New York City on a Saturday or Sunday lately? The line stretches out the door, and the cost of admission is expensive. People love beautiful art. We have original art in most of our guest rooms, not just the more expensive ones. Guests truly enjoy them, and frequently ask us about the artist. No one within our price range is doing this.

As someone who loves to cook, William Sonoma is one of my favorite stores. One of their hottest products is the Nespresso espresso makers. It is always prominently displayed in all their stores and catalogs. We have them in all the rooms. Many of our guests have them at home and are thrilled to see them in the rooms. Others have purchased the machines after trying the coffee at the inn. In my travels, I have only encountered these machines three times (once in Rome and twice in Canada). I believe that we are the only lodging establishment in New Hampshire offering in-room espresso.

Being a romantic inn, there is nothing better for setting the mood than great music. Right now about half of our rooms have Bose sound systems, and we plan to add more in the future as we replace older equipment. Most lodging properties have just cheap $17 clock radios.

The above are just a few examples of where we have taken the road less traveled to totally delight our guests.

It is interesting to note that all four inns/B&B in Sugar Hill have perfect five-circle scores on TripAdvisor, and yet none of them are my competitors in any significant way. Each property has found their own and nonoverlapping route to excellence.

Chapter 23

Being Famous—Living in a Fishbowl

No new book about hospitality would be complete without including a discussion of TripAdvisor. They are now the eight-hundred-pound gorilla of the travel industry.

As a kid, people were always commenting on my name. Now there is a whole generation that has no idea who Steve Allen was. I often wondered as a kid what it would be like to be famous. Fast-forward to 2006 and fame was not even on my list. I was moving to the small town of Sugar Hill, in rural New Hampshire, to enjoy a quieter way of life.

One week after buying the inn, we were having a strategy session with Marti Mayne on the front porch. Marti is the best public relations expert in the bed-and-breakfast industry. Marti told us that we had gotten a very negative TripAdvisor review that we needed to respond to. This was the first time I had ever heard of TripAdvisor. It was our first week, and these people wrote the most vicious review possible. I will admit that at that time, the inn was run-down, and we were inexperienced, and some of the comments were accurate. Other comments were trivial, such as our muffins were too small or out of our control, holding us responsible for the weather. We learned an important lesson that day. Anything we say or do may appear on the world wide web. Any anonymous person can say anything whether it is true or false. Getting inaccurate information corrected is almost impossible.

In those eleven years since 2006, TripAdvisor has become a major force in travel. In talking with my guests at the inn, most tell me that our good reviews played an important factor in their decision-making. Although almost everyone reads them, only a handful of guests take the time to write reviews. Fortunately, we have excellent reviews, and I would like to thank everyone that has taken the time to write a review. Reviews are also available on Yelp, Google, and Bedandbreakfast.com.

It is common for Karen and I to share a glass of wine together in the tavern after I have seated the last table in the dining room. Guests are always welcome to join us. For some reason that I can't explain, someone complained about this online. This is what I mean by living in a fishbowl. It was during our peak fall season when we were both working eighty hours a week. However, most guests are pleased to see that we get a few minutes to sit down.

"It's so pricey" is the number one criticism I read on TripAdvisor regardless of the property. I have a hard time understanding this since price was the one absolute fact known before booking. There is a basic law of business that must not be violated. A business that does not earn a profit won't last. The Sunset Hill House up the road from us went out of business as a result of always offering deep discounts. Sorry, we need to earn a living too.

Innkeepers have a love/hate relationship with reviews. While we love reading the good stuff, our obsession with reviews has a practical side. Innkeeping is how we earn our living. Good or negative reviews greatly affects our ability to earn a living and the livelihood of all our employees.

My wife, Karen, will tell you that I am obsessed with TripAdvisor. She is right; I do check it several times a day. There are two factors in play. One is that I am competitive, and that is how I keep score. The other factor is that I get great satisfaction in making people happy. That is what hospitality is all about.

Bad reviews can ruin my day or at least depress me for a few hours. In this competitive business, anything less than perfect is considered negative. However, after the emotions have calmed down, I would seriously analyze the content. Reviews that stick to the facts are the best. Some comments are too personal and inappropriate. I have been called names, and Karen's charming Southern accent has been mocked. We have made many changes based on feedback. An occasional guest who sincerely wants to help us by providing negative but caring feedback will do it discreetly on a comment card or send us an e-mail.

Now let me give you the inside scoop on TripAdvisor. No, it is not run by a retired Supreme Court judge with the unselfish goal of providing consumers fair and unbiased information. TripAdvisor is a hot stock on Wall Street, just like Facebook or Google. Their goal is to encourage as much content as possible, your reviews, that will generate traffic on the site, creating an attractive platform for advertisers. We pay over $1,800 per year, up from $800 a few years earlier, just for a tiny link to our website. They are earning millions of dollars from companies like Hotels.com and Expedia. By the way, we do not use Hotels.com, Expedia, Priceline, or similar services. They charge commissions of up to 30 percent to the lodging property. Even for properties that use these services, I recommend that you book directly with the hotel. You will be treated as a VIP and more likely to be upgraded and receive preferential service.

Have you ever wondered why some inns have more reviews than others? There are the logical reasons, such as some properties are larger. Those that have very negative or positive feelings are more likely to write. Also, when a property changes ownership, the old reviews are erased. For the most part, it reminds me of the electoral process. Inns, bed-and-breakfasts and hotels campaign for votes. Some properties campaign harder than others, and a few cross the line of ethical behavior. Friends and family are the first to vote. So unless a property has over twenty-five reviews, you are most likely reading the reviews of friends and family. If they have all stayed at the property, this is well within the rules. At the Sugar Hill Inn, we send a thank-you e-mail to every guest a few days after checkout and do include links to TripAdvisor, Yelp, and Bedandbreakfast.com for those interested in leaving reviews. Other properties are selective in who they ask. Afraid that asking everyone will do more harm than good. TripAdvisor has a new service that they are pushing hard that they claim to be very effective. It requires giving them guest e-mails so that they can badger you directly. This is a program that we absolutely refuse to participate in. We respect our guests' privacy.

An entire field of reputation management has come into being with high-powered consultants. We do not use any of their services. Our approach at the Sugar Hill Inn is simple. We do it the old-fashioned way, by working hard to see that every guest is happy. We focus on the small details in the hope of exceeding expectations. Our other method is what I call transparency. We have one of the most comprehensive website of anyone in the industry. An entire page is devoted to each guest room complete with multiple large photos. We even have pictures of most of the bathrooms and artworks. Anyone one who took the time to carefully plan their trip will find us exactly as described and pictured, leaving no room for disappointment. This book is congruent with our belief in transparency.

In spite of my obsession about reviews, there is another voice within that warns me to be careful. The Sugar Hill Inn is known for creativity and being innovative and wining a popularity contest sometime requires appealing to the lowest common denominator. We recently stayed at an Omni Hotel in Charlottesville, Virginia. From the point of view of an AAA inspector, it would have been perfect. The room was large, clean, had good lighting, a good bed, comfortable seating, and appeared to have been recently updated. Everything was a shade of beige. This so-called perfect room left me feeling totally bored.

In my early career, I was assigned a number of market research projects. Finding information on your competitors back in those days was hard. Now I can easily read reviews on all my competitors. Reading between the lines can paint a very detailed picture. I even read the reviews of noncompetitors to identify trends, to better understand guest psychology, and how better properties handle tricky situations.

It might seem like I am negative on the review process. The reality is that I have written over 140 reviews and use the site for my own vacation planning with relatively good results. It did disappoint me in Montreal. So my recommendation is to use the site, but beware of its limitations. It is frequently comparing apples and oranges. The $75 a night B&B might have a perfect score, but if you are a luxury traveler, you are not going to like it. The text of the reviews is often more important than the actual score. Look for reoccurring themes and people that you relate to. The concerns of young couples may be very different from that of older travelers or families with children. As a traveler, I generally read the negative reviews first, and I then look at the other reviews written by this person. If they are constant complainers or have little travel experience, I tend to discount their opinions. I think that consumers who do their homework in planning a trip are generally the happiest, and depending solely on TripAdvisor will disappoint. Do you trust your brother-in-law's recommendations or the neighbor down the street? Who do you think is writing these reviews? It is important to know that there is a silent majority that has never written a review and never will. While I would like to see more people write reviews, most people are just too busy or don't care.

However, our experience is just the tip of the iceberg. Now there are reviews for doctors, carpenters, professors, eBay buyers and sellers, employers, and every product imaginable. For good or bad, we live in the age of information overload. Everyone has an opinion, and as in politics, we frequently don't all agree. Going with the crowd might seem safe but is frequently wrong. All that I can say is that reviews can be a useful tool when combined with other information and careful thought.

For those of you who have stayed at the Sugar Hill Inn, we welcome your reviews.

Chapter 24

Maintenance, the Refrigeration Emergency

It was a hot August Saturday night. In the middle of dinner, the chef comes out of the kitchen to tell me the walk-in refrigerator was not cooling. We had a full dining room, a big breakfast the next morning, and hundreds of dollars of food that needed refrigeration. I confirmed the situation and placed an emergency call to our refrigeration repair service. This was not our first emergency call for this walk-in. After-hour repairs are painfully expensive, and that is always when things break. Dinner proceeded smoothly in spite of the refrigeration emergency. Everyone loved his or her dinner. The repairmen arrived within a half hour. We were pleased with the quick response. At first we were hopeful. A fuse had blown. After about thirty minutes, we were given the bad news. The compressor was dead and could not be fixed. He said that all the components were extremely old, and they should all be replaced, and he would work us up a quote on Monday, and it might take a few days to order the equipment. I said, "Isn't there anything that you could do tonight to keep the system alive for a few days until the new equipment comes?" He said, "No."

Continuous maintenance goes hand and hand with owning an older inn. Washers and driers run continuously. Things wear out; the riding mower needs service, and bees build nests where they shouldn't. While most guests treat the property with respect, others are just hard on the facilities. If you put your full weight on a towel bar as if it were a handrail, it will pull out of the wall, leaving a hole. We have been lucky in recent years. All the upgrades we have made to the plumbing, heating, electrical, and other system have meant fewer unexpected breakdowns.

However, this summer, our luck had run out. It started with the dishwasher. Commercial dishwashers are not like home units. Not anyone can fix them. Hobart comes all the way from Manchester, and the call is always expensive. The pump had failed. This is the most expensive part. We had a choice, almost $2,000 to repair or $4,500 for a new machine. Why are commercial dishwashers so expensive? They can wash a load in five minutes compared to the thirty or more minutes for a home machine. They also operate at high temperatures to sanitize in addition to cleaning and are built strong to handle heavy usage. The kitchen hood exhaust fan also died and needed to be replaced.

We had other problems this summer, but for now, let's get back to our story. Our chef, server, and dishwasher all worked late into the night to unload the walk-in and find alternative refrigeration. They commandeered both the wine and beer cooler in addition to the innkeeper's personal refrigerator. Some things we choose to freeze.

The next morning, we had a full house of twenty-six guests for breakfast. As usual, I was in at 6:00 a.m. on Sunday to make our famous crepes. Breakfast preparation was extra challenging because it was a scavenger hunt to find where everything was now stored. I had to take the cappuccinos off the menu because the workspace in front of the machine was taken up with all the beers pulled from the beer cooler the night before. I also pulled the English muffins with local jam from the menu because I could not find them. Since we had to use every square inch of the available refrigeration, fitting stuff in took precedence over our normal functional and logical arrangement of food. In addition to our usual tables of twos, we also had a table of five and eight to make the morning more challenging. Karen gave me a hand in the kitchen, and everything went out in a timely manner. Our servers reported back that breakfast was a big hit and everyone was happy. No matter how chaotic it might be behind the scenes, it is important that the guest enjoys calm, well-orchestrated hospitality.

The show must go on. I spoke with the chef, and he was confident that he had the resources he needed to do Sunday's dinner. We decided to honor all the reservations on the books and would have space for one or two additional reservation. However, we would not do our tavern menu. We grind our own beef for the tavern burgers, and we just did not have optimal climate control for this. Safety always comes first. Our 7:00 p.m. reservation canceled with only ten minutes notice. How rude! We had already told someone that 7:00 p.m. was not available.

Sunday afternoon our check-in arrived for the Dream Cottage. This was their third stay, and they came bearing gifts of fresh produce from their garden. How wonderful is that. They had spent a great day on their ATV (all-terrain vehicle) exploring the White Mountains. All they wanted was a quick dinner in the tavern, a great shower, and sleep. For those not familiar with ATV-ing, you are covered with dirt from your day of exploring. Karen had to explain to them that we only had our four-course menu and would not be doing the tavern menu tonight because of limited refrigeration. They were not happy.

I call the time between 5:00 p.m. and 6:00 p.m. the crazy hour. We are busy with check-ins, mixing drinks, answering questions, and welcoming dinner guests arriving early. At some point while I was running around, attending to my guests, the folks in the Dream Cottage called and left a message on the answering machine, saying that they had no hot water. I ran out to the utility room for the Dream Cottage, and sure enough, the gauge showed the water was cold. Now I had to explain to these people that we needed a service call and that it could not be fixed tonight. I did offer to move them to the Peckett Suite. They pointed to all their stuff and said they did not really want to move. They also reminded me that we had disappointed them with dinner. The Peckett Suite, our second best room, is only fifty feet from the Dream Cottage, but to our tired guests, it seemed much farther. Generally, it is our policy that if there is an issue with the reserved room, we will give a free upgrade if available. Unfortunately when you already have our best room, an upgrade is not possible. I showed them Peckett, and now they had the keys to both rooms.

A short while later, the man from Dream cornered me on the front porch and explained his disappointment. I politely listened and acknowledged his feeling. I said that we would not be charging them for the night, but there was nothing I could do tonight to fix the hot water in Dream. I had already called the gas company, and unless we had a gas leak, there was no after-hours service or even the ability to leave a message.

The next morning at breakfast, Karen checked on the Dream couple. Karen is better at handling difficult guest interactions. They had used the shower in the Peckett Suite but decided to sleep in Dream. Franconia Gas arrived early and quickly restarted the unit. However, they had no idea why it failed, and therefore, we could not be certain that it would not reoccur.

That morning we also called Vermont Heating and Ventilation to find out the status of the walk-in project. We were told the repair would cost $3,500 and that the parts were in stock at their distributor in Rutland, Vermont. I told them we had a very special birthday dinner on Thursday and needed everything to be working no later than Wednesday. They said that they would get back to us tomorrow. The chef told me that if he did not have refrigeration, he could not accept our food delivery and could not open for dinner. Mrs. G. over a month ago had made a reservation for eight to celebrate her sister's birthday. Disappointing her was not an option. A follow-up call on Tuesday assured us that the crew would be at the inn on Wednesday. In my mind, the odds of pulling off Thursday's dinner party was fifty-fifty.

Sure enough, the crew arrived at 8:00 a.m. and worked until almost 7:00 p.m. We were back in business, and Mrs. G. loved her dinner party along with the other tables that dined that night.

These are the issues that can stress me out the most as an innkeeper. When something breaks at an inopportune time, all I can do is to manage the situation the best I can. That means being open and honest with our guests, finding creative solutions, and pushing our vendors for the best service possible. With almost everything dependent on electricity (the well pump, refrigeration, reservations, etc.), we installed a backup generator several years ago so that we could maintain essential services in case of a blackout.

In response to the thank-you e-mail we send after every stay, the people in Dream said, "Thank you, we did enjoy our stay. While it didn't start out as we had planned, we appreciate your effort to make it right for us. Thanks again!" I was pleased with the outcome. We treated the guests correctly by not charging for the first night, understanding the problem from their point of view, and resolving the problem as soon as possible.

About a week later during a random check of Dream, I discovered no hot water again. Service quickly came and fixed the underlying problem. All this occurred while the Dream guests were out hiking and never knew of the issue.

While facilities management and maintenance are far from the glamorous side of innkeeping, they are vitally important. We have a huge investment in our facilities, and guest satisfaction requires great rooms. If someone is too hot or cold or can't have a great shower, we are in trouble. With new refrigeration equipment in place, I now have one less thing to worry about and lower utility bills.

Chapter 25

Four Diamonds

Marketing is all about having a good story to tell. Part of that story is our awards, reviews, associations, ratings, and designations. In this chapter, we are going to focus on the question, Is the AAA Diamond rating still relevant? We will also consider the importance of associations such as Select Registry and brand identification.

As a kid, I remember going to the AAA office to pick up maps, guidebooks, and a customize triptiks prior to any road trip. I know that there is a whole generation out there that has no idea what a triptik is or even cares about what the AAA has to say. Back in the sixties, there were so many independent mom-and-pop motels the AAA was really helpful in identifying quality places to stay. With the development of the branded chain motels, there was less need to check the guidebook. We knew what each chain stood for. For Holiday Inn, it was "The best surprise is no surprise." Chains such as Marriott, Hilton, and Sheraton were considered more upscale. Brands made selecting a place to stay easy. Fortunately, the boring sameness of the chains became evident to many travelers, and independent lodging properties have come back into vogue. This was especially true for bed-and-breakfasts and country inns. Once again, there was a roll for the AAA, but big changes were just around the corner.

Today with social media (TripAdvisor, Yelp, etc.), the relevance of AAA is under attack again. And for what it is worth, do people really care what Fodor's, Frommer's, Lonely Planet, or Rick Steves thinks? In defense of guidebooks, many of our international guests have found us in Lonely Planet. We will also take a look at the real story behind Bedandbreakfast.com's Diamond Collection.

The Sugar Hill Inn has a three-diamond AAA rating. We do not promote it because it is useless. Almost any halfway decent property qualifies. For most people two diamonds are scary. I won't deny it; I would love to be a Four Diamond property. It still carries a lot of prestige and would certainly be good for business. When our TripAdvisor score changed from 4.5 to a perfect 5 circles, it made a huge difference. It is not that the inn overnight changed but the hard work over many years was finally recognized.

Of my primary competitors, two of them used to be Four Diamond but are no longer and one still is. Karen and I have stayed at many Four Diamond properties across the country that are not nearly as nice as the Sugar Hill Inn. On the surface, there seems to be no rhyme or reason to who receives the Four Diamond award. At one place in North Carolina, the room had polyester sheets. I am sure that must be a violation of the standards.

My fellow innkeepers who do have Four Diamond properties I am sure will say that I am just whining, and that is the perfect lead-in to a story that might explain what is going on with the AAA and why the Sugar Hill Inn will most likely never receive a Four Diamond award.

> In Italy, most wines are known by where they come from, such as Chianti, Barolo, Montalcino, Orvieto, etc. To protect the value of these names, standards have been developed. Quality wines that meet the standards are given the designation of DOC or DOCG and the right to use the place name. Traditionally, everything else was thought of as cheap *vino da tavola* (table wine). On the surface, these regulations seem to be a good thing. These rules prevent someone in the geographic area of Chianti from producing an inferior wine, slapping on a label, and selling it as Chianti. However, these strict rules

were a hindrance to a new breed of winemakers who believed that they could produce some of the best wine in the world by growing international varietals such as Cabernet Sauvignon in Tuscany and blending them with Italian varietals. This was unthinkable to the wine establishment. For the longest time, these wines by regulation received no recognition and were designated as ordinary table wine in spite of their quality. Today these wines are known as Super Tuscan, and they are outrageously expensive, and Italian regulators have created a new designation called IGT to accommodate them.

In many ways, I feel like a Super Tuscan winemaker, unwilling to give in to the status quo. On a recent inspection, we scored 3.8. A score of 4.0 would qualify us for the Four Diamond. So where did we go wrong? To start with, you need to qualify your least expensive room. At the Sugar Hill Inn, we offer a wide range of rooms. We think that is a good thing. Not everyone wants the same thing when they travel. We have many guests that want to stay in an upscale inn because they enjoy great dining, the pool, and want to socialize with their fellow traveler in the tavern but spend very little time in their room and therefore are happy that we do have some smaller and less expensive rooms. Our smaller rooms still come with all the amenities, such as robes, slippers, espresso, premium bedding, etc.

We lost points because our bathrooms did not have artwork. For about $500, I could run out to our local print shop, and in a few hours, I could have cheap art in every bathroom, but that is not who we are. We are seriously committed to the fine arts. We have original art in almost every guest room and throughout the inn. The humidity would ruin a $1,000 painting, and cheap prints would discredit our program of original art. Even at very expensive properties, it is unusual to find original artwork in guest rooms. Our focus on original art is one of the unique features of the Sugar Hill Inn experience, and we are not going to compromise one of our core values just to earn an award.

All our bathrooms have premium hair dryers, and in most rooms, we have chosen wall-mounted units because we believe that these offer greater convenience to our guests. Personally, it annoys me if I need to search for the dryer under the sink, remove it from some fancy bag, and then plug it in. For some reason, that makes no sense to me. Wall-mounted units cause you to lose points.

Karen and I very carefully consider the design of each guest room. What will look best and be most comfortable for our guests? If a room has simple wooden blinds instead of heavy curtains, we are not being cheap. We like bright, airy rooms with clean lines. AAA will not look at the blinds within the total design context of the room. We will arbitrarily lose points because they prefer curtains. Real wood custom blinds frequently can cost as much as curtains.

According to the AAA, a hotel room should have two comfortable chairs. When we purchased the inn in 2006, all our rooms met this requirement. In many rooms, the chairs were not in close proximity, making conversation difficult, but the number crunchers at AAA were happy because we had two chairs. Being a romantic inn, we believed that couples would want to sit together, and therefore we replaced many of the chairs with love seats, causing us to lose points. Once again, arbitrary standards are more important than the overall guest experience.

I could go on all day with examples. Let me give one more. Most of our bathrooms have framed mirrors, but some are unframed. Here again if we have an unframed mirror, it is because we think it looks best in that particular room. In many of those rooms, we have chosen to use very expensive natural stone tiles, but fancy tile does not earn extra points. I am also not aware of any hotels charging under $500 a night with Nespresso espresso makers, but if the luxury is not on the checklist, it does not count. Being innovative is penalized in the AAA system.

I could certainly walk around the inn with the AAA playbook and do a lot of small stuff to placate the AAA inspector. The question is, would following the playbook make us a better inn? In all honesty, the answer is no. Of course, even if we did pander to the system, there is no assurance that we would receive the designation. The true value of the designation is in keeping the club small. I believe that it is predetermined that we will not qualify for the Four Diamonds before inspection. Although they have worksheets with numerical values for every category, this kind of work can be very subjective. We all know the saying "Figures don't lie but liars can figure."

Not all diamonds are real. That is how I feel about the Bedandbreakfast.com's Diamond Collection. This is pay to play. There is a difference between a marketing program and true recognition of achievement. Bedandbreakfast.com runs one of the best and most comprehensive website directories for bed-and-breakfasts and country inns. There is an excellent chance that your Google search for "New Hampshire B&B" has taken you to Bedandbreakfast.com. The Sugar Hill Inn has always paid for placement on the site. About five years ago, they came up with their Diamond Collection program. For a substantial extra fee, they will promote your inn as part of this exclusive collection and get you premium placement on the site. We use the program because it works, but it is not an exclusive group, and almost anyone can qualify. To qualify, you need to be an inspected property. Since the AAA automatically inspects most properties and a three-diamond inspection qualifies, this requirement is not as restrictive as it sounds. As we discussed prior, this is a huge group with those at the bottom being pretty average. They also look at the reviews on their site. A 4.0 out of 5.0 is good enough for them. In my mind, most good properties are in the 4.5 to 5.0 range.

I have presented a dilemma. AAA Three Diamond is such a large group the score is meaningless. AAA Four Diamond overrates some properties and totally misses many fine inns. Bedandbreakfast.com's Diamond Collection is nothing more than feel-good marketing. In a previous chapter, we discussed TripAdvisor and the review sites and how they frequently compare apples and oranges. So is there a safe, dependable way to select a place to stay that will work time after time?

My father had a saying, "You will be judged by the company you keep." This could not be truer than in the lodging industry. The Sugar Hill Inn is a proud member of Select Registry. As a member, we are subject to surprise undercover inspection. Although each member's property is unique, the Quality Assurance Program makes Select Registry the most reliable way to select a place to stay. Select Registry also keeps its members up-to-date with the lasted trends by sponsoring meetings, webinars, and trade shows. There are other associations, such as Relais & Châteaux, that are also known for quality.

If you are curious about the difference between Select Registry and Relais & Châteaux, this is how I see it. Select Registry properties, while upscale, are still relatively affordable to most travelers. Relais & Châteaux properties are a little bit more exclusive and priced above the budget of most travelers. There are many Select Registry properties that could qualify to belong to Relais & Châteaux but prefer membership in Select Registry. There are also similar associations for larger independent hotels such as iPrefer. Karen and I stayed at a wonderful iPrefer hotel in Bermuda called Cambridge Beaches. These associations should not be confused with brands like the Ritz-Carlton. While investor groups may independently own the real estate, they are operated as Ritz-Carltons by Ritz-Carlton management. Some smaller chains are operated under the franchise model.

I have said this before, but it is worth repeating. We are all different in what we look for in a place to stay. A place may be highly rated and a quality property in every way, but that does not mean that it is the right pick for you. Guests who do their homework are the happiest. As a lodging property, we give as much information as possible to make the task of homework easier for the consumer. If you are booking on Hotels.com and by passing the wealth of information on the lodging property's website, you are doing yourself a disservice.

Chapter 26

Is Airbnb a Threat to Traditional Hospitality?

If you own an inn or B&B, being the innkeeper is just one of your jobs. You are also the chief executive officer. It is your job to navigate the ever-changing economy, competitive landscape, social trends, rapid technological change, and to dodge the power of the ever-changing giants of the travel industry. Once-powerful companies like Kodak and Polaroid are gone because they failed to anticipate and keep up with change. Just because your B&B is cute and located in the most tranquil town anywhere, you are not immune. However, don't let this scare you. Change creates opportunity. You could easily become the new number one in town because the former market leader is afraid to change the strategy that made them so successful ten years ago.

In my eleven years of ownership, I experienced the financial crisis, the rise of online travel agencies (OTAs) and TripAdvisor to industry dominance, the change from desktop to mobile, and how Facebook has become an everyday habit for most Americans. Many believe both Facebook and Google have big plans for the travel industry. I am proud to say that we have done well in this environment.

I say the above to put the worry many innkeepers have about Airbnb into perspective. As individual innkeepers, we have no ability in influencing market forces, but that does not mean that we can't have very successful strategies to deal with these forces. As B&B owners, we have always been niche players beyond the reach of the giants. There are good reasons why there are no fourteen-room Ritz-Carltons. With their huge corporate overhead, they could never make the economics work.

Wikipedia defines Airbnb as follows: "An online marketplace that enables people to list, find, and rent vacation homes and apartments for a processing fee. It has over 1,500,000 listings in 34,000 cities and 191 countries." Airbnb was founded in 2008, and I first heard about it in 2011 from my millennial-generation daughter. At about the same time, I also learned about Uber from her. At that time, she was living in New York City and said I should stay at an Airbnb when coming to visit. It would save me a lot of money. At first, I didn't even know what she was taking about. Once I understood, I still was resistant. The last thing I wanted to do was stay in some stranger's apartment. Besides, I have always liked hotels and the services they offered.

While I may have been resistant to trying something new, Airbnb grew exponentially. In cities like New York, Boston, or San Francisco, if there is a major trade show in town, hotel room become hard to find and very expensive. There was money to be made. If you have a well-located apartment, list it for a few nights, sleep on a friend's couch, and come home $1,000 richer.

Since my daughter, Sara, now lives in Washington, DC, sometimes we will just pick a fun and interesting place to spend some family time together. I gave up sharing a room with my grown daughter a long time ago. It is just awkward. We have guests who do that at the Sugar Hill Inn. I understand getting two hotel rooms becomes very expensive. Last year we selected Los Angeles for our trip. To keep the cost down and to better understand this trend in travel, I agreed to give the Airbnb concept a try. We used another company called VRBO, but the concept is the same. Expedia owns them. If you think there are a lot of hotels in Los Angles, looking at vacation apartments and houses was overwhelming. I sent lots of e-mails inquiring about specific properties, and most of those e-mails were never replied to.

I decided I wanted to experience one of those homes high up in the Hollywood Hills. I found the perfect two-bedroom house with magnificent views for under $500 per night. Two hotel rooms at a nice place would have cost more. Online I sent in an availability request that was soon answered. A $50 cleaning fee was added to the bill along with a rental fee. I believe that there was also an option to buy insurance. The house also required a $1,000 security deposit that was promptly refunded after checkout. This was a different experience then staying at a hotel or B&B. Without GPS, I would never had found this place. The nearest restaurant or store was a fifteen-minute somewhat stressful drive down the mountain. Fortunately, the prior guests had left behind some coffee. Daily housekeeping was not available. On our last day, as we were about to leave for the airport, we could not unlock the garage to get the car out. When something goes wrong at an Airbnb, there is no front desk to call. Fortunately, the owners were very responsive, and we did not miss our flights. The house worked perfectly for Sara and me, and I did get to experience life in the Hollywood Hills. However, when traveling with my wife, Karen, I prefer the service and amenities that a hotel or inn provides. If I were in the area again, I would want to stay at the Beverly Hotel.

If you listen to innkeepers, it seems that Airbnb is their number one concern. There seems to be two issues. In some markets, Airbnb has dramatically increased the supply of properties available to traveler. Increase supply puts downward pressure on pricing. The second point is that there is not a level playing field. Many Airbnb owners are part of the underground economy. Not paying required taxes, violating local zoning, not having commercial insurance, or not meeting the same safety and fire codes. Because this business has grown so fast, lawmakers have been slow to respond. As zoning laws are enforced, commercial insurance required, and taxes are collected, these inequities will fade. There are many communities that do not allow short-term rentals of less than six months.

Airbnb is not for everyone, just like staying at an inn or bed-and-breakfast is not for everyone. Some people are just happier at a

Hampton Inn, where every hotel will look and feel the same from coast to coast. There is one issue that does concern me. My thinking has always been that inns and B&Bs provide a truer local experience than a big hotel or motel. Airbnb has taken the local concept to the next level. Both their website and expensive television ads proclaim, "Live there . . . Experiences places like you live there . . . Don't go to New York, don't go to Paris, don't go to LA—live there." I encourage everyone to watch the video; it is super compelling.

Let's answer the important question. Has Airbnb had any effect on the Sugar Hill Inn? My answer is no, although the situation may be different for other inns or B&Bs. We specialize in couples with an average stay of two nights that want the amenities of a full-service inn. The economics of renting a house favor larger groups and longer stays. Hotel rates in the White Mountains are low to average. It is the lure of high returns that incentivizes many homeowners to flood the market with their properties. Being in rural New Hampshire, being a full-service inn gives us the advantage over both a bed-and-breakfasts and rentals. There are no coffee shops, markets, and restaurants across the street. Staying with us makes it easy. Enjoy wine with dinner and just walk back to your room. The town of Sugar Hill has always had a lot of vacation homes, and that has not changed.

The travel industry is huge. Camping, renting a motor home, cruising, budget hotels, expensive hotels, resorts, vacation homes, bus tours, B&B, country inns, boutique hotels, etc. Staying in a rental home is not new. The White Mountains are full of vacation rentals. Airbnb has not invented the rental market. It has always been there. Just like the way Expedia, Hotels.com, and Priceline, for good or bad, have revolutionized how hotel rooms are booked, Airbnb has done the same for the vacation home and apartment market.

Let's end this discussion by taking a step back with a story. Tennis has always been popular, but in the late seventies, early eighties, there was a tennis craze. New indoor tennis clubs popped up everywhere. Billie Jean King and Chris Evert were household names. Everyone was taking tennis lessons, including myself. Five years later, those new indoors clubs were mostly gone. People who always loved the sport are still playing. People like me with no talent for the sport moved on a long time ago. I am sure that there are still famous tennis players, but they are not household names in my family. The rise and fall of tennis did not affect America's love of sports. In fact, the sports we play and follow are more diverse than ever. I believe that Airbnb, while offering some additional choices to travelers, will not replace the more traditional avenues of travel.

Chapter 27

Lessons Learned

In May 2006, when I purchased the inn, it was just one of many average and somewhat tired country inns with its glory day a fading memory. The previous owners were smart, hardworking, and friendly but had a business model that was wearing them out, leaving little family time, benefiting only the mortgage company and the inn's suppliers, and leaving little money to reinvest.

Only someone wearing rose-colored glasses could consider risking it all on this money pit. I remember bringing my girlfriend up for the weekend before buying it. Standing on the Forest View deck, facing the rear of the inn, her eyes were focused on the deteriorating roof, peeling paint, and the herculean task of turning this place around, while I was focused on the inspiring views of Mount Lafayette, the historic farmhouse, and the pride of owning fifteen of the most beautiful acres in the state.

No matter how much research, planning, or thinking you have done, when you sell your home, move to a new state, and buy an inn, you are venturing into the unknown. Although my vision of enjoying cocktails on the front porch and lounging by the pool was far from reality, I have no regrets.

Now eleven years later, the inn has been renovated, and occupancy has more than doubled; the inn has been featured in numerous publications and has received awards from Distinguished Restaurants of North America (DiRōNA), Wine Spectator, Yankee Magazine, and New Hampshire Magazine. The inn also has a perfect score on TripAdvisor, Yelp, and BedandBreakfast.com. This has been an amazing journey.

Not only did I change the inn, the inn changed me. Some people are lucky; they know what they want to do from a young age. I struggled to find a career that I really enjoyed. I found what I was looking for at the Sugar Hill Inn. Over these eleven years, I have become more confident, a better leader, wiser, and yes, older.

It is ironic that while I was creating the perfect romantic getaway for others, I found Karen, my true love. The Sugar Hill Inn would not be what it is today without Karen's significant contribution and role.

The other day, I was enjoying one of those rare moments sitting at the pool. I was being a guest at the Sugar Hill Inn. I was enjoying the view, the tranquil sound of the waterfalls, beautiful landscaping, and eyeing a magnificent inn. I could not resist thinking that Karen and I along with the rest of the team had created a very special place.

My wife will be honest and tell you that being an innkeeper is not a normal life, and she is right. In some ways, it's like show business. You are always on stage, and you live for the applause. We love sharing the good life with our guests of fine dining, great wine, beautiful art, and stylish rooms, but behind the scenes, we have lots of rooms to clean, mountains of laundry, and a payroll to meet. One minute we are living the lifestyle of the rich and famous, and the next minute we are pulling weeds. This profession is not for everyone, but I have enjoyed it and would do it all over again.

If you are used to a steady paycheck, this will certainly be different. We earn most of our income between June and the end of October. October is a fantastic month, but it is important to squirrel money for those slower months. On the positive side, living at the inn means very little in personal expense (no personal mortgage or utility bills, etc.). The workload is also unbalanced. We work hard in the summer, and it's crazy in the fall. The rest of the year, the workload is mostly concentrated on the weekends. We take off ten days in

November and three weeks in April. Some inns take longer vacations, but we find that it is hard on our staff if there is no work.

Being an innkeeper is more a lifestyle than a career or a job. If I have a great conversation with someone in the tavern, am I working or socializing? If I am adding a new Bourbon to the bar, am I working or indulging an expensive hobby? Karen and I love to travel and dine out, but at the same time, we are always analyzing the food, room, service, wine, etc. So many of our conversations revolve around the inn. Just the other day, Karen and I were dining at a local restaurant and, by our standards, identified four service errors. One, never remove the silverware from the plate you are clearing and return them to the table. Two, don't bring out the entrées when the guests are still working on the appetizers. The third point had to do with the wine service, and at this point, I can no longer remember the fourth service error. However, the food was good, and we still enjoyed our night out and generously tipped the server.

To the surprise of many, it takes a staff of twelve to run the inn. Karen, the chef, and I are full-time, and everyone else is considered part-time. Keeping these jobs filled with hardworking and motivated employees is our biggest challenge. Sometimes it seems like everyone who wants a job already has one. I try not to talk politics at the inn. It's a loaded subject. However, our biggest competitor when looking for new employees is the welfare state. Working too many hours means losing partial disability, winter heating subsidies, free health care for the kids, student lunches, food stamps, etc.

Seeing the inn go from average to what many guests describe as a gem to me has been so satisfying. Every business owner will tell you that there is a lot of hard work behind his or her success, and that is true. However, I can point to many hardworking people in this profession that have not been successful. It is important not to forget that you are running a business. For a business to last, it must turn a profit. Business is about managing risk. If uncertainty keeps you up at night, find a nine-to-five job. As in many businesses, the eighty-twenty rule applies. If you are not familiar with it, 20 percent of your efforts will produce 80 percent of the results. Of course, the tricky part is figuring out where best to spend your time. Being a full-service inn is much more complex than being just a simple bed-and-breakfast, but I enjoy having control over all the aspects of hospitality.

I think that it has worked for me because I have been able to combine solid business management with creativity and my love of travel, great food, hospitality, and design. I didn't know it all on day one, but I love learning new things, and I do learn something new every day. I just finished a book on the history of bourbon and, as a result, have added a couple of new ones to our lineup.

I also needed to step up to new challenges. Most innkeepers are very outgoing by nature, but that is not me. It is my personality to be quieter. I had to push myself to step up to the challenge, and I believe with good results. Every once in a while, someone will score unfriendly on the comment card and that is discouraging. Unlike some inns, we do not hug our guests.

Turning around the inn required hundreds of decisions and actions. Some were large, and some were small, but they were all important. There was no magic bullet to propel us to success. I also need to say that good ideas are a dime a dozen. The real challenge is implementation and to consistently follow through day after day. We were not throwing ideas at the wall to see what stuck. We understood that we were an upscale romantic escape known for gourmet dining and stylish rooms. Decisions had to be congruent with who we were.

Building the Dream Cottage was our biggest, boldest, and smartest decision. The Dream is our best-selling room and the most expensive. What a great combination. Back in 2007, while I certainly believed in the project, I had no way to know for sure we would be so successful. Jim Collins, in his best-seller, *Good by Choice*, presents the concept of "fire bullets, then cannonballs," and that is what we did. Bullets refer to low-risk activities to see what works. We tested the waters of upscale accommodations by redecorating the Peckett and Richardson Suites with good results. Seeing that we were on track, we built the best upscale luxury guest room in the White Mountains. In other words, we fired the cannonball.

While creativity and original thinking is certainly an asset, you do not need to reinvent the wheel. Show me a struggling innkeeper, I will bet that they rarely travel, belong to trade groups, or attend innkeeping conferences. By belonging to trade groups, you will quickly learn who are the best photographers, web developers, etc., that specialize in serving B&Bs and inns. You will also quickly learn who some of the better vendors are. Believe it or not, when attending industry conferences, 80 percent of the program is technology. Understanding websites, search engines, reservation software, booking engines, Google Analytics, social media, e-mail marketing, online directories, etc., is more important than your grandmother's secret soufflé or brownie recipe. It is vitally important that the Wi-Fi reach every room and even work at the pool. Yes, Wi-Fi is a necessity that people can't live without. If technology is not your thing, there are plenty of consultants to help the confused.

When traveling, stay at the best. You are not going to learn anything new at a Motel 6. As a Select Registry inn owner, you can stay at other inns within the association for 50 percent off. Many inns will be glad to trade room nights. Some places you will need to pay full price, but it will be worth it. To see hospitality at its best, I recommend the Inn at Little Washington (Washington, Virginia), Auberge Saint-Antoine (Quebec City), Boston Harbor Hotel (Boston, Massachusetts) and Hotel La Cep (Beaune, France).

Back in my college days, I was an economics major and remember studying about the famous economist Adam Smith. In his groundbreaking book *Wealth of Nations*, he introduced the concept of the invisible hand. The invisible hand of the marketplace/economy reaches deeply into every business for good or bad.

A good economy lifts all boats, and a bad economy is like swimming against the current. We had to deal with the financial crisis of 2007. American Express just arbitrarily canceled all its small business lines of credit. People were reluctant to spend money on luxuries such as going way for the weekend or fine dining. Spending money on expensive wine became politically incorrect even if you could still afford it. It was a scary time for small businesses. Although we were successful in spite of the economy, I am sure that it did significantly impact us.

For many Americans, owning real estate has been their road to building wealth. I purchased my first house in my midtwenties. At that time, interest rates were 17 percent, and the housing market was dead. As rates fell over the next few years, the value of the house took off like a rocket. I plowed the profits from that house into my next home, where I lived for the next eighteen years before buying the inn. Over those years, the property appreciated threefold. I was not a real estate genius. Anyone who owned property in the New York, Los Angeles, or San Francisco metro areas had similar results. My inflated house became the source of the down payment for the inn. While there are many factors that determine an inn's value, certainly the underlying real estate is a major factor. The value of the inn has grown over the years due to new investment and much stronger business performance, but the underlying real estate so far has not contributed. I am not discouraged. Almost all the appreciation in value with my second house happened after the tenth year. When a market turns, prices can move up fast. Based on discussions with area Realtors, our market is warming up. Regardless of appreciation, every month my mortgage payment is building equity.

The final lesson is not to forget that the decision to become an innkeeper was more a lifestyle than a career decision. Innkeeping is 24-7. While profits are necessary, profit maximization is not. It is important not to answer the phone after a certain hour. There are crazy people that will call you at 3:00 a.m. We have an answering machine for messages, a website with everything you need to know, and online reservations for both the inn and restaurant. It is not unusual for some people to try to negotiate down our rates in the off season. We appreciate an occasional day off and certainly do not want to trade it for a half-price room. Set aside days for hiking and sightseeing. Enjoy coffee on the front porch, the pool, and occasionally being a guest in your own restaurant. Having experienced all the local attractions and restaurants will make you a better innkeeper. Tuesdays and Wednesdays are date nights, so someone else will be watching the inn. It has become tradition at the end of a long day for Karen and I to share a glass of wine and great conversation. We are fortunate to have a great wine cellar.

I have enjoyed telling my story. To the curious, I hope that this behind-the-scene look into innkeeping will enhance your future travels and the appreciation of the art of hospitality. Every innkeeper has a story to tell, so as you travel, engage your host in conversation. Ask to see the other rooms. I love showing off our inn. If you have a favorite inn, write them a review; they will be very grateful.

For those considering buying an inn, I have tried to paint a balanced picture of innkeeping. For the right person, this profession can be exciting, fun, and challenging. Every lodging property is different. Look for an opportunity where you can build on the best of the past and bring new energy, ideas, and money to assure continued success.

If you are currently an innkeeper or owner of another type of small business, reread the chapter on being the best in the world. While the goal might be elusive, pondering that question and working in that direction will pay big dividends.

To all my readers, thank you for visiting. If you were staying with us, I would send you home with fresh-baked cookies.

The End

ABOUT THE AUTHOR

Steven Allen graduated from the University of Denver with a BA in economics and earned his MBA in management from the College of William and Mary. After years in the corporate world and a successful entrepreneurial career, he earned a diploma from the prestigious French Culinary Institute and then bought an inn in rural New England. Steve and his wife, Karen, own the Sugar Hill Inn, a Select Registry inn. Their property has won numerous honors, including Wine Spectator's Award of Excellence and Top Ten Romantic Inns in the US. The inn was featured in *1000 Places to See before You Die* by Patricia Schultz. The Sugar Hill Inn is open year-round as a luxurious getaway in the beautiful White Mountains of New Hampshire. Steve is an innovator, bringing fresh ideas to hospitality and making the inngoing experience relevant to the next generation of inn goers.

Chaine Des Rotisseurs, the world's oldest international gastronomic society, has awarded Steven Allen the title of maître hotelier. Steve is actively involved in the community and has served seven years on the board of directors of the Franconia Notch Chamber of Commerce. He is also a founding member of the Association of Independent Hospitality Professionals.

CPSIA information can be obtained
at www.ICGtesting.com
Printed in the USA
BVHW06s0858300518
517702BV00006B/11/P